AFTER THE FACT
Scripts & Postscripts

AFTER THE FACT
Scripts & Postscripts

Marvin Bell and Christopher Merrill

WHITE PINE PRESS / BUFFALO, NEW YORK

White Pine Press
P.O. Box 236
Buffalo, New York 14201
www.whitepine.org

Publication of this book was made possible, in part, by grants from the Amazon Literary Partnership; the National Endowment for the Arts, which believes that a great nation deserves great art; with public funds from the New York State Council on the Arts, a State Agency; and with the support of the Office of the Vice President of Research at The University of Iowa.

Acknowledgments:
    #1-10 *Denver Quarterly*
    #11-20 *Conversations Across Borders*
    #21-30 *The Georgia Review*
    #31-36 *Ecotone*
    #37-42 *The Iowa Review*
    #43-52 *Prairie Schooner*
    #53-58 *Fiddlehead*
    #59-60 *december*
    #61-70 *The Georgia Review*
    #71-80 *december*
    #81-90 *The Georgia Review*

Cover image: "Against Perfection" by Sam Roderick Roxas-Chua, used by permission of the artist.

ISBN: 978-1-935210-88-7

Library of Congress Control Number: 2015959242

Table of Contents

Preface / 9

Scripts

Postscripts

Preface

After the Fact: Scripts & Postscripts began as a sequence of sixty paragraphs written back-and-forth with Christopher Merrill over a period of fifteen months in 2011-12. Having written sixty, we decided to go on to a second section. Hence, the subtitle, *Scripts & Postscripts.*

Chris and I first met in 1978. It was Chris, aware of the back-and-forth poems I had written with William Stafford—a series published in 1983 as *Segues: A Correspondence in Poetry*—who suggested we try something like it. It was to be thought of as poetry, but we decided on paragraphs which, it seemed, might better embody a wide range of experience and imagination.

Chris has undertaken cultural diplomacy missions for the State Department to more than fifty countries. Hence, while I sent my paragraphs from Iowa City, Iowa; Port Townsend, Washington; and Sag Harbor, New York, Chris sent his from Uruguay, Chile, Russia, the Congo, Uzbekistan, Afghanistan, Mozambique, Zimbabwe, Vietnam, Cambodia . . . .

Given the nature of Chris's experiences and my predilections, as the sequence pushed ahead it took up matters philosophical, sociopolitical and aesthetic. The title *After the Fact,* as well as the original working title, *Everything at Once,* now seem apt characterizations of an international, postmodernist, digital age.

— M. B.

I

Scripts

CM:
Reunion

You know the story: how the child disrupted the banquet, parading around the tables during the welcome address, knocking over water glasses before the toast to the former director, curtseying under the lectern until the keynote speaker decided to cut short his remarks on the meaning of success. *Quite a performance,* the hostess said as he left the stage. She smiled at the delegates, some of whom had traveled great distances to celebrate their good fortune—the fact that in their youth they had chosen to dedicate their lives to a cause which in the fullness of time proved to be more fruitful than they had ever imagined possible. The child was standing on her head. *We must do it again,* the hostess said to close the evening—and that was when the fun began.

MB:

Joe

We were gathered in a student apartment in New Orleans for the Mardi Gras, an enticement to lure us to a writing festival of old pals afterward. I took a couch and went to sleep early. I wanted to locate the Zulu parade the next morning. That night, I dreamt of my old schoolmate, Joe Elephant. He lifted me in his arms in a bear hug. I liked Joe Elephant, a big person but not, as many were, a bully. I had not thought of him in years. Such a good memory suddenly from small town schooldays. All day at the parades, I remembered Joe Elephant. How a memory may surface without a visible prompt is a mystery for scholars of neurons, relays and the illusion of time, but habitual for poets. How happiness is its own reward, yet must be located. My own happiness continued for several hours until I realized I had never known anyone named Joe Elephant. By such mental shenanigans have I held the string of a balloon, and by such indirection have I been lifted, as one might be by nothing but syntax, where inner and outer worlds intersect. Of course, my Joe was the person I had known as Arnold DiCarlo, but I digress.

CM:
The Red Balloon

The soloist broke a string in the last measure of the cadenza, and
in the silence that fell over the lawn outside the amphitheater a
child, letting go of her red balloon, shrieked in despair. Of the
families picnicking in the shadows cast by the setting sun there was
one unhappy couple folding paper plates into a garbage bag, each
blaming the other for their disappointment in the festival program-
ming, the selection of guest artists, the conductor's banter with the
crowd, and now they stopped to watch the balloon sail toward Dol-
lar Mountain, which this summer they had climbed too many times
to count, never pausing long enough at the top to take in the
view—the tall peaks surrounding them, the valley stretching south-
ward to the horizon . . . . The orchestra waited as the violinist tight-
ened then tuned a new string. The child ran to her father,
demanding to be lifted onto his shoulders before the balloon dis-
appeared from sight. What did the couple feel? Relief? Some things
are better left unsaid. Another music filled the gathering darkness.

MB:
Burke

James Burke, the one-armed cornet virtuoso in the Edwin Franko Goldman Band, performs his nightly solo in Central Park, then makes a token move to return to his seat but turns and walks back out front to add an encore. Roger and I are up front and have followed the sheet music to the solo where Burke could see our dismay when he skipped the optional high obbligato. Burke steps up every solo a notch to where you can hear the holes in the valves and pipes lining up with tiny, rapid explosions of spit and breath. I'm a son of the Fifties, the raw emotion of doo-wop, the *schmaltz* of Harry James, the flutter tongue of Clyde McCoy, the high register of Cat Anderson. The oboists like to take apart their instruments and blow through the reeds and keys while Goldman glares. You don't forget a thing like that. From such time-travel has come this moment, which began six decades ago to arrive just now. It never ends. It might be *wah wah* on a plumber's helper, or Kenton's big band brass doing the *shakes*. It was a fine time to be the trumpeter Shorty Rogers, but that's another story.

CM:
Aztec Two-Step

I saw them at the Bottom Line—or was it another club? What grieves me is that I can't recall if anyone was with me. Did I go into the city by myself? At fifteen I knew how to hitchhike to Morristown to catch the Erie Lackawanna to Hoboken, take the tube to 34th Street, and get a beer at Burger & Brew before heading to the Village. But did I really go alone? The war in Vietnam was winding down, and my father had given me his draft card from the Korean War to use for ID. No one checked, though I was small for my age; also solitary. Which may be why I found a table close enough to the piano to see what *a couple of papish cats doing an Aztec two-step* looked like, whatever Ferlinghetti meant by the lines printed on the album cover. I liked the sound of his words, though, and the duo's harmonies. They never had a hit, but they still perform at folk festivals and private parties. In fact they outlasted the Erie Lackawanna: bankrupted by Hurricane Agnes, which destroyed miles of tracks, and the completion of I-80, which cut into the freight business, the railroad was sold off, the commuter cars with the wicker seats replaced. One day I would drive straight across the country on that interstate, playing "Highway Song" over and over to stay awake. In my memory it was the last song I heard at the Bottom Line, probably because of the refrain: *Nothing matters now except the dawn.* I left after the first set—and somehow missed the last train in Hoboken. Which meant that I had to sleep on a wooden bench in the station. Was I afraid? Certainly. Alone? Ask me another time.

MB:
Code

In a small town, everything is elsewhere. My memory of radio remains lodged in Morse code. That's how we went from here to there in those days. Roy's ham radio shack was his attic. Herb's was his backyard repair shop. Van's was a one-room house in the woods, where he built transmitters only to see if they worked, one after another. The smell of solder glued the walls, and a dozen dials glowed to measure space. Memory, like the fabled primordial ooze, lies shapeless at a murky depth. It may emerge in the form of a boy's twenty-watt call to the far world, it may live again as a whiff of smoke or solder, or as a song at highway speed, and it may hold a kind of code. My memories go their own way. Some are too personal for words. Some are just dry storage. But oh my, the ones that still matter—if one can crack the code and read between the lines. The old telegraph operators could "copy behind," and would let the Morse message run on ahead while they packed a pipe or retied their shoes. Just so, the years run on ahead, but memory catches up. Morse code has been phased out, like muscle memory over time. It was years before I knew that Dorothy puts herself to sleep by silently reciting poems, state capitals, the ninety-nine counties of Iowa . . . . Yet she has tried to learn International Morse code and cannot. So she says. I suggested she learn the dots and dashes for the day when I might have a stroke but be able to blink my eyes in code. I think this reason has something to do with her not being able to learn Morse code. Love is the child who closes her eyes to make things go away. And to relive the past. I heard three times from Saint-Pierre & Miquelon Islands.

CM:
The Score

Hope 5, Stars 0: this is how a revolution begins, with a blowout on the soccer field and a young woman falling in with the mourners of a man who set himself on fire. His coffin sails above the chanting men, who must bury him before the sun goes down. *Five-nil*, she murmurs like a prayer as the crowd approaches the square guarded on three sides by riot police. The man next to her repeats the score to the boy sitting on his shoulders, who tells it to his cousin, who sings it to his uncles, who take up the refrain, pressing forward, bolstered by the rising voices. So codes develop—a phrase taking shape in one imagination is passed to someone else, and soon everyone is talking about the same thing, the language tuned to a new frequency. Jars of preserves are hauled out of dry storage and bottles filled with water for the long night ahead. Why did the man take his life? A policewoman slapped him in the face. The players ran off the field.

MB:
Frankie

They arrested the poet for inserting the phrase, "a pig in boots." They testified that it wasn't poetry. They said everyone knew who he meant. A candle forever sputtered in the church where the hero of their past had forged alliances. My host walked ever more slowly around the lake until the others were far ahead. Only then would he mention the protest. The meeting was on. The writers' union newspaper was set to shout at the government. He could not know as he spoke that the Party editors would resign from the editorial board, undoing the required quorum, and the paper never appear. Nor would one republic help another. They each had their own language, ethnic foods, facial bones and hair dyes. They won their credentials with patriotic books, extolling the leader. They translated prodigiously, but only from abroad. At public events, the poets of beauty drew rolling applause, the synchronous thunder of mass agreement. Protest took the form of imaginative fictions, nuance and allegory. Quick digs in the ribs of the rulers, laughs at their expense, the half-hidden early stages of rebellion. Every dissenter a majority of one. I think of Frankie, my childhood friend from across the street. Late in a short life, he opened a tattoo parlor. "You should see my arms," he told me.

CM:
Prayer Rope

He needed no training for the special work assigned to Frenki's Boys—his murder conviction had won him early release from prison—and in the lobby of the Grand Hotel in Podgorica, on the eve of a civil war that never came to pass, he took pleasure in describing the clearing of a village in Kosovo: the raping and pillaging, the breaks for tea and cocaine. He looked high (bloodshot eyes, trembling hands), and when he winked at me, twisting the black knots of his prayer rope, I looked down, pretending to read over my notes. The faithful are instructed to silently recite the Jesus Prayer as they count the thirty-three knots worked into the rope (one for each year of His life), and if it was hard to imagine this paramilitary praying to the Son of God, his loyalty being to a man destined for the War Crimes Tribunal at The Hague, I could believe he hoped for even more rewards in the next life. At the next table were three businessmen speaking in hushed tones. I made a mental note that they were probably as well armed as my jittery guest, who had more stories to tell, which I did not particularly want to hear. But I took down every word of his testimony. What did He say about the tax collectors? *Those who are well have no need of a physician, but those who are sick* . . . . Now I remember how the prayer ends: *have mercy on me, a sinner.*

MB:
Kenny

Before news broke in pixels, before time-shifting, when telegrams and long distance calls were alarming, we watched out the window. That was where people gave themselves away. Mornings, Mr. Johnson went by on his walk to the bank. Increasingly, he walked with a stoop. The war was bending him in two. His son sent a snapshot from the front. Kenny sat behind sandbags and a fifty-caliber machine gun. By the time the picture arrived, Kenny had run out of bullets many times. The Kenny who came home from Korea was another Kenny than the one who had gone overseas. Inside most of our homes were photos of the Pope and thick paintings of clowns and Native Americans, and of western scenes done by sponge and putty knife, the air over the plains dusty from migration. To us, that was far away. Wartime was teaching us geography. There was talk of interstate highways to better move the troops. If, as it had been said, there could be no poetry after The Holocaust, there would be no weakening of our search for the transcendent. The weather on our island obeyed few laws. Many sent an invisible balloon into some version of an afterlife. The Main Street wall of local war dead had room for more names.

CM:
Stories

Driven from the island first by high winds and then by debt, they devised new rules for their vacations: never revisit a place; never travel by the same means from one year to the next; never apologize; never tip; never tell anyone their destination . . . . The children could discern no pattern in their trips to Gettysburg, the Grand Canyon, the Mall of America. Nor did they know why the stories their mother told to the proprietors of the inns in which they stayed bore so little relationship to the facts as they knew them—they did not own a wooden boat on which to sail around the world; their father would not join them for the fireworks on the 4th . . . . Of the island they remembered chasing ghost crabs into the dunes, and poking a Portuguese man-of-war washed up on the beach, and sitting on the rafters late at night to watch their father read. How they loved the iron grating on the drawbridge, and the dried seaweed they draped around their babysitter, and the juices spurting from cracked lobsters. They hated green flies, and the red flag waving above the lifeguard station, and the way a blowfish swelled when it was out of water. They could not imagine not returning. After all, the house swept out to sea had been rebuilt, and though it had to be sold they still believed they would return one day. What stories would they tell then? Once there was a house . . . .

MB:
Sylvester

Sylvester made a bee sound in the back of the classroom, humming while he did the dance of the zipper on the fly of his pants, purring while he ran the zipper up and down, as if he might have been Leroy "Slam" Stewart humming as he slid along the frets of his standup bass, though Sylvester didn't know of Slam Stewart. We lived on individual islands, each to our own music. Many chose never to cross the canal that separated the halves of our actual island, or to go to the Big City of new citizens and first generation Americans. Sylvester liked to say, "Well, tickle my wig." Was it funny, defiant, sexual? He said it in wonder or dismissal, he said it to friends and teachers, he said it when he had nothing else to say. Then he'd return to the dance of the zipper while the teacher rolled a map down over the chalkboard to show that there were other places. If all rhetorical questions were to be answered, if infinity and fantasy did not undercut language, if one could know what another was thinking, then there would be logic to the narrative of a life. I heard that Sylvester was killed by a truck at the dump. That was the story.

CM:
SOS

Facetious, my mother liked to say, pronouncing the second syllable with extra stress, schooling us in irony—which according to the latest studies children can understand by the age of four. *I'm being facetious.* What I heard was sea, and indeed the tidal motions of language, the wit lurking in the hidden currents of a word or phrase, are bound in my memory to my mother's surges of humor. *Facetious,* she said one night by the stove as if to herself, buttering the toasted bread over which she would ladle creamed chip beef—the one dish that my father taught her how to cook upon his discharge from the army. He had taken the test to be an intelligence officer and ended up in the kitchen, where he claimed to win the battle of Pork Chop Hill—another joke that sailed over my head. *What's for dinner?* I asked. *SOS,* my mother said. *What's that?* I said. *Save our ship,* she said. *Save our souls.* My father let slip another meaning: *shit on a shingle.*

MB:
Nat

The laughter and ribaldry of those on the front, the humor of those who survive, the comedy after narrow escapes. We have clowning, we have tomfoolery, we have slapstick, we have farce. We are ready to put on a show. We have routines to overcome the back stories. On the funny side of grit, one may find in one's memory an organ grinder suffering his working pet's shenanigans on the lower east side of New York. One may honor the likes of Nat, who was known to entertain the wounded troops at the veterans' hospital, Nat who had a patter and some hijinks that brought him accolades. We gathered for his appearance on the *Ted Mack Amateur Hour*, and there was our own Nat, my uncle, his bald, unpowdered head like a sun in the flickering black and white of our television. The band accompanied him as he hummed "For Me and My Gal" through kazoos shaped like a trumpet, a trombone, a clarinet . . . . We had expected more of his act, but the veterans welcomed his good heart, on top of which they did not require talent. It was Nat who took me to the museum. He said he was an FBI agent who left his badge and gun at home on weekends. Naturally, my favorites at the museum were the dinosaurs. In truth, Nat was a janitor at the New York studios of Warner Brothers. Saturdays, he was his own cantor in *shul,* and he was apt to sing at the drop of a hat.

CM:
Greystone

I never knew why she volunteered at the state hospital for the insane.
Nor did my mother know if she met Woody Guthrie there (the pa-
tients' names were kept secret); the mythology surrounding Dylan's
visit to the singer, a young artist paying homage to a master, lay in
the future, along with the madness of Vietnam. Her favorite story
concerned the man who introduced himself as George Washington
and asked her to save his cookies for Martha. She told him he would
likely see her before she did, since his winter headquarters were just
down the road. But he would never leave Greystone, a bucolic cam-
pus with the largest building in the world until the Pentagon was
opened. Woody Guthrie was another story. He was neither a drunk
nor insane—he had Huntington's disease, a genetic disorder little
understood in those days, and eventually his family moved him to a
hospital in Brooklyn. What we inherit—traditions, inclinations. The
treatment of the autoimmune diseases passed on to me my doctor
describes as an art—which is to say: no one knows why the body
will attack itself. In 1964, Dylan's bewildered fans called him crazy
when he picked up an electric guitar. Last night I watched a docu-
mentary about his transition from folk singer to rock star: at a con-
cert in London a man called him Judas. *I don't believe you,* Dylan said,
and instructed his band to play louder. Another man told him to
go home. Home? The original buildings at Greystone, once home
to thousands of poor souls, are slated for demolition. Dylan's end-
less tour has taken him back to Europe this summer. *This land is your
land,* my mother sang.

MB:

Mr. Pople

August, and the music of the spheres has been wrapped in an ocean of Air Force engines on night maneuvers. When they roll across the ceiling we feel a rumbling like that at the edge of a storm, bordering tornado or calm—and we wait. The music of the spheres, a radiant sense of proportion, if inaudible, to the Greeks, is this night the rocketry of the heavens. A relentless drone, a tinnitus that has driven men insane. Just as no nation can win a war from the air, or defeat a populace that believes they are fighting for their own land, so the shrinking of our silence proposes a worldwide lobotomy. As formerly we leaned into the pregnant silence, now we carry the afterthoughts of news. A mechanic sucked into a jet engine said he didn't feel it. A skydiver whose main chute did not deploy landed on his feet and survived. A family man whose boat broke up in shark waters made plans to sacrifice those who floated away from the group. After they all pulled through, he had a lifetime of guilty nightmares. Mr. Pople, our school counselor, wounded in the war, walked on a wooden leg. His stilted gait made us look away. He kept our IQ scores private, lest we endure the expectations of parents. Just so, we hear the jets overhead and feel smothered. When they turn back toward the base, a relentless ocean in our ears ceases its motion. The tide at its turning gives us a moment of inward peace. Mr. Pople's tests suggested our fitness for jobs we were unlikely to find. He knew we would likely stay where we were. It is the work of philosophy to teach us how to survive ourselves. Sometimes, it is hard to think anything.

CM:
The Lake

At daybreak, wrapped in a blanket on the porch of a cabin by a lake, I look up from a history of the twentieth century to see mist hanging above the calm water, the bands of green—cedar and fir and spruce—that define the mountain blocking the sun, an osprey nest crowning a lodgepole pine on the far shore, like the knob of a walking stick. No wind. Only the stream trickling into the lake, and then the sounds I am learning to distinguish here: the hum of a dragonfly, the splash of a trout leaping near the dock, the whistle of the train bound for Whitefish. From the sealed freight cars families were separated into lines of men, women, and children, then stripped, shaved (their hair was used as stuffing for mattresses and wigs for dolls), and led to the showers, sometimes to the accompaniment of women prisoners singing arias from the railroad platform. Now a woodpecker needles a tree by the portage to the next lake, and from the bunk bed inside the cabin comes the sighing of my older daughter as she shifts in sleep. Now the nest under the eaves springs to life— the chirping of three chicks eager for the worm brought by a robin that alit above me as I read about the women raising their arms so that their children could fit into the shower with them. The mouths of the chicks will remain open after the robin flies off.

MB:
Staircase

If one had never fallen down a flight of stairs, perhaps there might have remained, and I say this with a smile, might have remained a sense of the stairway as an abstraction, a roadway in the air, a corridor too advanced for walls, in a society in which one could be forever safe while acting naturally. One's first thoughts would still encompass all of the present moment, instead of the infinite number of traces, nuances, hints, flickers, flitterings, and floaters impinging on one's mind from other days and places, some of which may have long since ceased to exist. Such are we who feather our landings with a last grasp at what is not there. In this way, the current of one's sensory awareness slows down as a collision of any sort begins to approach. A few seconds will take a long time during a smashup. By long and short divisions of time we make of the continuum of our lives, not to mention the neural pathways of thought, paths befitting the corkscrew, the chambered nautilus, fictive Klein bottles, and traversable wormholes. Using the half-step and the stutter-step, the pause and suspension, we choose where to place a foot, and another. So it proceeds, a presence lost to entropy, as the wind flattens our footprints, the tide washes them away, and we learn, as we hurtle, spinning, from the landing to the floor that the way we came is not the way back. The apparitions of truth are forever bound to the fears of a parent. Try not to think of what you wish to remember.

CM:
Breach

Half of the stairway vanished in the storm surge, which flooded the barrier island, freed a fleet of fishing vessels, and gave rise to a new political class defined by its singular inability to govern. It took months for repairs to begin on the drawbridge, no one could agree on a plan to reopen the lighthouse, and the sand accumulating in the inlet, the result of a hasty decision to close down all dredging operations, brought an end to shipping. The merchants were preparing to take matters into their own hands when funds to protect the sea turtles dried up; soon a pit lined with broken eggs appeared on the beach, among heaps of sea wrack and driftwood, buoys and crab traps—and then the tourists returned. On their first morning the children ran down the boardwalk from the rented house to what remained of the wooden stairway, and there they found only air. They stood on the last step, astonished, daring each other to jump into the dunes. He had a red badge pinned to his bathing suit, she wore a white hat and blue sun dress. Below them were patches of sea oats, holes into which to chase ghost crabs, timber and masts from shipwrecks. Wild horses galloped along the beach, which was not as wide as they remembered, and they had never heard such a clattering of waves breaking over the ribbon of shells along the shore. A dolphin breached the glittering sea. The boy turned to the girl. *One, two, three!*

MB:
The Dock

On islands of a certain configuration, those who had paying jobs stopped each day at the dock on the way home to make sure the bay was still there. They sat and looked out. They turned their car radios down. It was no longer possible to draw in crabs by the bucketful with one's high beams. The clam forks now brought up more and more trash. Where a drop line had sufficed, one needed a long range motor to carry the lines to fresher seas. Such collateral damage notwithstanding, water's edge still held a memory under the current, a trace of origins, and a residue of wreck. If one lingered, the ghost of moody Neptune might begin to bubble up. Now the task of grandparents was to keep alive those who had passed on. Each day, the workers drove home by way of the bay, then roads around the inlets, some with a stop at the ocean beach. Without sufficient drainage, rain pooled on the roadways. The creek water sighed as it passed. The tide turned tail and took to sea what one was just about to pick up. The Old Country of their elders was water over the dam. The origin of species went no farther back than that of extended families. One hoped the children might live nearby. Survival skills change over time, and one of them is living in the past.

CM:
Combs Hollow

I liked the sound of it, and the fact that we went there after dark, on the eve of the parade, led by the bellowing of bullfrogs from the creek to the reservoir, through wet grass and reeds, until the music stopped. I held my breath, my father lit a cigarette, mosquitoes swarmed around us. In the silence before the advertisement calls resumed I searched the ground for slivers of mica from the abandoned mine and arrowheads left by the Lenni Lenape, the Real People forced from this land before the Revolution. The frog that I mistook for a rock refused to jump, not then and not the next day when the floats built for the 4th of July circled the viewing stand at the community center and then the contests began: firemen climbing ladders, turtles on the baseball field. Combs rhymed with tombs in our village, which was divided among dairy farmers, blue-collar workers, and commuters to the city, executives like my father, who was stricken that day by the heat and had to be taken to the pool to cool off. Nothing I said or did could make him move.

MB:

9/11/01

Since the autumn of 2001, film editors have been erasing the image of the World Trade Center towers from the New York City skyline. They do the task readily, running the software with which they soften skin, enlarge biceps and bosoms, and eradicate the native imperfections of our species for the look of magazine covers, book jackets, personal websites, and concert flyers to be stapled to light poles or wedged under car wipers. They change bodies, nature and cities. They lop off childhood and old age, they give the infirm back their young legs, they fix warts and outsized appendages. They make smiles wider. The edited will live forever on the Internet in the place of whatever was or happened. The towers lodge now in a pixelated and pixilated cosmos that makes no distinction between the terrible and the tacky. Attempts to restart the past include platoons of pagan exorcists slow-walking in a round, circling to acquire the centrifugal force that will shed evil. Drums and rainsticks, whistles, shakers, pedal notes and falsetto, rap and scat—all have sorrowed and defied. By such links to what happened is one made to focus, lest nothing make sense and the whole spin out of control. I remember how clean were the coats of the police and firemen. Majestic, even.

CM:

9/11/11

I ran that morning along the boardwalk by the Río de la Plata, which is either a gulf or the widest river in the world. High winds overnight had cleared the sky, and the street was empty save for a pair of men drinking mate by a parked car, stirring yerba in dried gourds with the flattened sieves known as *bombillas*, thermoses of hot water tucked underarm. A woman overtook me in a black track suit, and as she ran down the steps to the beach my heart soared. *Only temptation is divine*, said André Breton after resurrecting the writings of the Comte de Lautréamont, who was born and raised in Montevideo, during the war with Argentina. But I didn't follow her—I had to catch a flight to La Paz, with an intermediate stop in Santiago, where student protesters were marking another anniversary: the coup d'état that brought General Augusto Pinochet to power—and on the way to the airport I consoled myself with a memory of the French consul's house, from the balcony of which young Lautréamont likely witnessed the siege. Antiques were for sale on the day I visited the square below the poet's window, and on one table, among old coins and tea cups and a gramophone, was a rifle dating from the war. Breton said the ultimate surrealist act would be to fire a revolver at random into a crowd: a whimsical idea that others developed into a military tactic, the governing principle of our time. We live in the shadow of terror, as Chileans live with the knowledge that in the end Pinochet escaped justice for his crimes against humanity. We, too, seem determined to ignore the excesses of our War on Terror— another misnomer, like the Río de la Plata, the coffee-colored Silver River, which behaves like an estuary. But estuaries must be protected from environmental degradation, which might cut into the maritime trade, and so it remains a river. No one wants to admit the truth: *Evil rebels against good,* wrote Lautréamont. *It cannot do less.* If only I had followed that woman running down the beach!

MB:
Aesthetic Wobble #1

Myth and history record certain omens beneath the comings-and-goings of mechanical and scientific advancement, looks back and catch-ups, and the general syncopations of planetary life nearly indiscernible under what we cheerfully call "the music of the spheres." Talking fancy is fun, too. We might take as omens the facts that the quantum physicist can't catch up to the past nor can one catch one's breath in hyperspace. An international neurosis, bent to the battle between subversive good and the ruling dominion of evil, festers in binary. The daily news is like candy at Day of the Dead parties—it erodes our bite. Breton today would be a maker of bumper stickers: "Arm the Poor." "Help the Economy. Buy a Senator." A siege of young protestors has been at the throat of Wall Street investment houses. Crossing the tracks on what was named, of course, "Railroad Avenue," my childhood dentist's car stalled and would not restart. There was a train approaching. Now *that's* an omen. While we wait, we make new distinctions and undo old ones. For example, it is an omen if it coalesces around a shiver. It is not an omen if it is merely precocious like pepper. It is an omen if it heats a kettle, but not if it clouds over. It is an omen if it billows, but not if it girds to cope. It is an omen if lush, but not if lifeless. It is an omen if it goes uphill, but not if it rents Parnassus. It is an omen if it recovers the Egyptians and Tibetans, but it is not an omen if it ends up language.

CM:
The Unwritten

In those days I took as an omen a flotilla of hot-air balloons sailing at dawn toward the Sangre de Cristo Mountains. And once I read in the upside-down flight of a bluebird a history of my soul: how it steadied its wings above the ruins of a great house built by the ancestral Pueblo people, in the still air of a canyon lined with caves, to glide over walls and plazas and kivas, unaware of the ceremonies and stories that defined the space below, the trade in shells and feathers, battles won and lost; how it inscribed in the sky a straight line from my past to the future without regard for the junipers and piñon pines about to burn up in a wildfire; how it embodied the silence of what would remain unwritten. In the disappearance of those tribes of which little is known I discerned nothing that applied to my circumstances, and twenty autumns passed before I hiked again in the mountains above Santa Fe, in a grove of aspens nearing the end of their life cycle. It was late in the afternoon when the trail merged with a logging road, and there I was struck to the quick by the sight of the golden leaves against the blue sky, which brought to mind the story of a child on the reservation drinking from a spring contaminated by tailings from a uranium mine. Omen or emblem? I could not tell. And indeed I began to wonder if I had invented that story in order to light some obscure region of my memory. I did not move until the sun had set.

MB:

Skippy

Two weeks underground after the collapse, the Chilean miners decided to asphyxiate themselves to end their suffering. Before suicide, the plan had been cannibalism. They were down to half a teaspoon of tuna per man every forty-eight hours. Then a probe broke into their safe room. Each one rose then through the miraculous technology, up through the afterlife that must attend every horrific occasion, into that day-by-day transcendence that is mankind's own creation. We hoped that they would experience the charitable entropy of the brain and the good fortune of the imagination by which one may blur, and even undo, the topography of horrid memory. The happy past hovers, and the dreadful goes underground to rot away until stirred. But not if one was there. It's black lung in the mines and black ops above ground, memories of which are split into those who were present and those to whom it was reported. People came back from Vietnam, from Iraq and Afghanistan, and said it was not worth it. Those receiving the medals appeared to know that, as heroes, they were the emissaries of cannon fodder. The miners, too, were cannon fodder, as were those who built the great cathedrals, the Pyramids, the Sphinx. Each person must answer the question, "To whom does my life matter?" The Classics will not tell us. We who survive may do so in the transformative manifestations of aesthetics while staying off the target, keeping our heads down, and affecting a goofy but likable demeanor at the far ends of late night subway cars. Trying to take the gun from Tommy, my easygoing pal Skippy shot off his brother's leg. Lacking art, what now? If one wants to be left alone, it's best to talk to oneself.

CM:
Fodder

A friend once said that writers are just fodder for the language. His long view of literary history (reflecting, perhaps, his disappointment over the sales of his last novel), raises the question: To whom does my work matter? Heretics burned at the stake, soldiers in the trenches who continued to believe in the nobility of war as they climbed the ladder to certain death, lovers who persist in sickness and in health—they may inspire either awe or bewilderment. Reserve your pity for the prisoners forced to march across the minefield, in the cruel joke of the tyrant who outlived all his enemies, the descendants of whom now occupy his palaces. The apprenticeship served by his stonemasons differed only in kind from that of craftsmen dating back to the discovery of fire: one must learn to hew and cut and polish precisely, with the tools at hand; to build things that last (foundations, monuments), one's love for the materials must outweigh the sometimes harsh conditions in which the work is undertaken and embody the knowledge that shrines to any deity, including language, acquire different meanings under the impress of wind and weather. Time will tell what will endure. Hence the tradition that Socrates was the son of a stonemason lends credence to the idea that in his arguments we see him polishing truths, which teach us how to live and die. To what do we pledge allegiance? The statue toppled after the invasion inflamed the imagination of the tyrant's friends and foes alike.

MB:
Celebrity

We felt famous when the dictator of an island nation purchased a waterside hotel in our bayside village and surrounded the property with high, alarmed walls. Long rumblings of the poor had made his circumstance shaky. We saw that he could arrive at the estate by boat, unseen. The presence of him and his florid spouse grew in our imagination. We did not expect to see them at the diner or attending the occasional fund raiser. Nonetheless—and I must interject here the palpable disgust we felt for his rule—the possibility, however faint, felt to us like fame. The star of a notorious pornographic movie, one long celebrated for its leading lady, in retirement had married a local carpenter, so there was hope. In school, we memorized what towns were famous for: shoes, fire engines, a prison . . . . If someone made the news, there could be a temporary suspension of judgment in the flare of celebrity. Something to talk about. Just so, documentaries hypothesizing the building of ancient wonders, elaborate constructions of levers and pulleys, and the brute chain of laborers amazed and mystified us. Who knew the Mayans knew so much? Of course the Philippine dictator never used the property.

CM:
Yasnaya Polyana

The guide wasn't interested in the diplomatic fallout from William Jennings Bryan's decision to postpone an audience with the Czar in order to extend his visit with Tolstoy. She preferred to measure the writer's fame in the number of pilgrims drawn to his country estate. Thus in 1903, with war looming in the Far East and new pogroms underway, Bryan and Tolstoy, united in their concern for the peasantry, rode horses, walked over the fields, discussed non-violence. Nothing justifies the use of force, said the Count, not even if a child's life is in jeopardy. The politician concluded that the secret of his global influence was love: "his shield and sword"—which, it occurred to me, might be useful in the practice of cultural diplomacy, the art of winning hearts and minds: my reason for traveling to Russia. Under the yellowing birches lining the driveway, the guide reported that Tolstoy had spent seven years of his life on horseback, and at the door to his house I was still tallying my years in the air. In his study I examined the encyclopedias, the Remington, the calendar of quotations (Ruskin, Confucius) opened to the day of his flight from Yasnaya Polyana. Schoolchildren tramped through the hall, with blue plastic booties pulled over their shoes. Above both beds in the rooms reserved for visitors were racks of deer antlers; in the ceiling was the ring from which Tolstoy planned to hang himself, just before his conversion. The Czar would assure Bryan that his government had nothing to do with the pogroms. Seven years later, thousands of journalists waited at Astopovo train station for word of the writer's death, which made the front pages of newspapers around the world. Imagine. How many children died in the massacres? Love is not enough.

MB:
Afterward

They who had been to Poets' Corner in Westminster Abbey, and to Thomas Hardy's Dorset cottage, now planned to dig up Shakespeare, but only if he had written the plays attributed to him, so they waited for a definitive announcement. Meanwhile, they debated whether Yeats was a pawn or Eliot an anti-Semite. They were searching the past for examples of a great writer without an unforgivable flaw, even one of those vices against which a slight resistance would have sufficed. Their thoughts were displaced from context and thus were the bitter conclusions of those condemned to forget the past. I myself was surprised at the arduous climbing Yeats must have endured on the stairway of the dank castle to which the future would make pilgrimages, ignoring the poet's plea to pass by. Inside Robinson Jeffers' tower, I mounted a spiral stairway, hidden within a wall, to the roof where the poet could see, then, an unobstructed Pacific. And old Eliot, having Groucho to dinner, wanted only to talk of *Duck Soup.* There have been times for truth, charity, humility, good cheer, fantasy and decency, even if the times were not most of the time. Poetry after the Holocaust—yes. As for the Czar and the Bolsheviks, then and now, a plague on both their houses, the very curse the Bard put into the mouth of the dying Mercutio, for whom neither the love of Romeo for Juliet, nor of Juliet for Romeo, would be a balm. Language being reductive, it is perhaps ill-advised to judge a person by what he or she says. Despite the sign in an overgrown section of San Michele Cemetery, I was unable to find Pound's grave on San Giorgio Maggiore. I went looking because I had once received from a poet snapshots of Pound's room in St. Elizabeth's Psychiatric Hospital with the clear implication that she had visited E. P. for intimate purposes. One must imagine the epic that was Russia during the reign of the Czars: grist for the mill, artistry in the air and the poor underfoot. My father died young. Had he stayed in Russia, he would have died younger. We visit the graves seeking longevity.

CM:
The Fountain House

The long years in the communal flat, across the courtyard from the palace, with her ghosts, her packed valise, her lover's wife steaming fish in the kitchen. There were informants everywhere. And in the walls, from which hung paintings and photographs, an icon and a pair of wooden skis, were listening devices. From the silence she monitored came a requiem for her generation: *Can you describe this?* On her table were letters, her son's identification card, drafts of poems. *I see it all at one and the same time,* she wrote: a definition of poetic vision. From her window I saw a white cross and, through a scrim of red and yellow and green leaves, the last rays of the setting sun; my notes revealed nothing of the emotion I felt among the things of the woman Stalin called *our nun*; the picture I took of the three crones minding the museum didn't turn out. But that night in my hotel room, when I finished packing, I found a grainy photograph of Akhmatova posing on a marble sarcophagus, like the Sphinx. *Man* is one answer to the riddle of her poems; *day and night* is another. The fate of her brilliant artist friends—glory, madness, suicide, execution, exile, death—didn't escape her lucid gaze. Sleep before my flight at dawn was out of the question.

MB:
At the Point of Death

Between the dreadful detail of the normal and the blur of the paranormal lay an abyss of emotional *in extremis*. The young Ukrainian boys dug trenches so they could reach the bodies between shellings. They hid in the forests to evade conscription or severed their trigger fingers. They went AWOL from the front lines. Then they left for the New World. Artists recorded the imprisonments, exile, madness and suicides of the famous, creating a flame in the midst of the horrific, while the peasantry ran, leaving behind anything that could be traced to them. They sought anonymity. They went to the movies to learn English. They had garlic parties in their strap undershirts and toasted life in Russian, but said nothing of the past. If you tell, someone finds out. They experienced everything at once. Their children, like all children, believed the world into which they were born was the normal one. The exponential pace of change would not be, for the new youth, a bareback ride to steerage and safety, but a walk in the park. The story goes that a large corporation experienced a computer problem for which it needed help. The tech guru who showed up was only sixteen years old. However, he could not solve their problem. They needed a thirteen-year-old. Someone with tunnel vision. Someone who was not yet himself. Another someone who would outlive the moment.

CM:
The Bridge

And so they spent another night in the mountains, in the spirit of the proverb: *It is permitted you in time of grave danger to walk with the devil until you have crossed the bridge.* The soldiers in the ravine taunted the snipers on the ridge, launching flares that landed in the river; tracer rounds lit up the sky in recognizable patterns, recorded by the fortune teller attached to the regiment; the signals man passed out rusks of bread confiscated from the monastery in the valley. In his pocket was a leather pouch containing sharks' teeth collected on a barrier island before his deployment; these he liked to count after dinner, mindful of his mother's warning about tunnel vision—which he understood to be a hazard of the trade, an unintended consequence of war. He also knew it might be necessary to destroy the bridge, which was heavily guarded; if he was reluctant to obey the order to betray the location of his best friend, who was calling in air strikes from the timberline, nevertheless he sent the garbled message that led the enemy to surround the last stand of trees, leaving their left flank exposed. This had been predicted long before he tried to pass off another man's words as his own: *Thus goeth the body . . . .* Yet what remorse he felt owed more to differences in strategy than to his friend's fate or his role in the operation. The monks assembling for the first office of the day would extend their fast. A shark will lose tens of thousands of teeth in its lifetime. The bridge remained in the sights of both sides.

MB:
Carlyle

Carlyle, our beloved dandy, working the post office window in bright suspenders, notices that the package is addressed to my sister in a rehabilitation ward. "Poor Ruby," he says. "What has happened to poor Ruby?" Dorothy explains that my sister has suffered a stroke. Carlyle is up to the task. "This planet," he says, "is a death trap." I remember thinking something similar as the tracer bullets passed overhead where I crawled the combat infiltration course. The bullets, we knew, "wanted our asses," and as such were reminders not to stand up, a topmost layer of absurdity—the icing on the cake of il-logic being the fact that I was crawling toward the machine guns, not away. Flares lit up the night to remind us not to run in the light. We had been taught it was crucial to shoot back. We had run bay-onets through straw men. A web of foxhole buddyship held us in place whenever it seemed right to bolt. Philosophy comes to the sur-face in P.O.W. internments and home front veterans' wards when one realizes that time ends. Yes, time. That hypothetical curvature that may yet prove to be tautological. An army bites its own tail. The stroke victim walks like a child. We are back on the battlefield, the night sky going intermittently bright, the thudding and whizzing of rifle fire, the whistling of artillery, and we advance while the nurse wipes our mouth and pulls the sheets up to our chin. A hopeless moment is still a moment.

CM:
Conference

The divinity students returned to the subject of a just war, which had caused such a furor at the conference on the separation of church and state. Their ailing classmate's intervention in the plenary session—a question for the cardinal about the veracity of his memoirs—had drawn a sharp rebuke from a philosopher renowned for her defense of torture, which they tried in vain to reconstruct—to the consternation of their friend, who kept adjusting his breathing tube. They stood in a semicircle around his bed, in a room at the VA hospital, debating military law: can you conscientiously object to one war and not another? What constitutes a proportional response to an act of terror? Their friend had interrogated prisoners in Iraq, and his systematic dismantling of the philosopher's argument, which endeared her to conservatives, was a thing of beauty. When he lay back against his pillow, chewing slivers of ice, the Augustinian in the group began to hold forth on intentionality, inspiring jokes about his refusal to read anything written after the thirteenth century. The one preparing for the priesthood dipped his fingers in a glass of water and wiped them on his trousers. An intern stopped by to say hello. The sun was setting, but no one thought to turn on the lights. The sick man described the tests awaiting him, his theory about the cause of his illness, the treatments available to a veteran. He was remarkably lucid; also tactful. He waited until the Augustinian had finished straightening the books piled on his bedside table—a treatise on phenomenology, a biography of Hemingway, a novel by Murakami—to signal that it was time for them to go: the nurse was at the door, with his pain medication for the night.

MB:

Aesthetic Wobble #2

If the patient did not moan while reaching for the morphine drip, if the suspect did not scream under the whip, if the eyes of the soldier did not freeze as the bullet pierced him—absent such sensory apprehensions, the image arrives as Surrealism, Dadaism, Objectivism, Imagism—ideas about art. They are as distant from the body as a toilet seat hung on an art gallery wall. They have the ephemeral effect of performers whose art is safe revelations in museums or on klieg-lit stages—body art, stasis, confession . . . . Warfare includes an Aristotelian catharsis for the home front. Not to be dismissive, it was likewise artistic skill that drew painting and sculpture toward the sublime for which it once strove and which in past centuries was endowed in the service of religious fairytales. An art for children's books, created by the Masters. An art of such exquisite proportions that it could paint the horrible as a stepladder to paradise. The human condition, so richly textured it shone with the full palate of sensation. Yet it is the smell of torture, as much as the look and sound of it, that defines it. Let the visions of the religious coalesce around the bedsides of the mortally injured, it can't hurt. Poetry, for its part, is unable to abandon its cosmetic surgery of misery and privation. That lovely word, "privation." Someone will stage it and call it a play.

CM:
Fairy Tale

He collected every fairy tale from the village at the end of the valley except the one he wanted—the story of a dancing bear, a peddler, and a woman, which had haunted his dreams in childhood and dictated his course of studies at the university. Emblazoned in his memory was the image of the bear chained to an apple tree whose roots had curled around the coffin of the mayor; he could not recall any other details of the story beyond the rumor, widely circulated, that it was based on an actual incident, and still he lost sleep imagining the consequences of eating the fruit gathered from that tree; hence his resolve to record the fairy tale in full, preferably in the lilting voice of his grandmother, dead these many years. (He blamed his insomnia on her juxtaposition of tone and subject.) However, his family had long since moved away from the village, the tradition of storytelling died with the burial of the church under a wall of snow, and no one could answer his questions: Who trained the bear? Did a peddler really lock a woman in a barn and hide the key under an altar? What taboo had the mayor violated by selling off the forest that protected the village from avalanches? He died before the last stand of pines was cut down; the whereabouts of his skeleton remained a mystery—which led the folklorist to speculate that privation, not magic, was the true source of this ghoulish tale. What consolation he took in the prospect of an afterlife was tempered by the knowledge that he did not know how it ended. If it ended.

MB:
The Evangelicals

The evangelicals came knocking on the door, wearing wings. I said I don't do business on the porch, and I'm not a candidate, but the leader spread his cape to reveal his inner being, which he took to be the truth he wished to share, while I took it to be his spindrift armpits. I lived on an island which caused me to think of sand and mud, whitecaps and anchors, droplines and worms. He had his eye on a planet toward which he was climbing on the backs of converts. He was headed upwards while I was going down. He had resuscitated the prophets. He had rolled away the rock to see who was alive in the cave. He had tallied the books and memorized the verses. He had logged the names on gravestones for soul-saving. This is what he lived for. He shouted on paper. He beseeched at the precipice, and blew like a foehn. He had broken the ancient code using only coins and yarrow stalks. He was as confident as the slave of a guru. He had come by way of disbelief and was now fervent in the embodiments of the spirits. He was every church and every Sabbath. He had his hands on the gold. His belief blanketed the roofs and washed away the daily paycheck. I had only a government in shambles to match his paradise.

CM:
After the Workshop

Mr. Vonnegut, a woman said before the last workshop, *I've never seen a dead body.* The novelist replied, *Just wait.* Meanwhile the janitor, an economist by training, vacuumed the stairwell in the parking garage, cursing the dry wind coming off the mountain, thick with dust and the voices of the missionaries lost on a star-crossed expedition— three old men who could not keep up with the reconnaissance team sent out at dusk to guide the planes dropping humanitarian supplies behind enemy lines; their prayers reminded the janitor of the equations corrected by his thesis director, which were in fact connected to the laws of supply and demand. *Try again,* the professor advised— words the janitor repeated as he emptied the vacuum cleaner. There was nothing more to say about the story of the lost mission—the woman realized that, yes, it was only a sketch, an idea to be developed, perhaps, in another medium—and so the novelist dismissed the class. The students made their way outside in time to see the funeral cortege of a soldier killed by friendly fire begin to circle the block. A trumpet blew, the crowd emerging from the church surged toward the riot police at the entrance to the park, and over the base of the monument to the unknown a priest poured from a silver bowl the blood of the lambs. *Just wait,* he said.

MB:
Luxury of Circumstance

He began to believe he might not have been present when the revolutionary army came down from the mountains to occupy the island capital, since the age of naïveté was by now so far past that his saying he knew nothing of the situation when he went there for the erotic exoticism for which youth pines now seemed like fictive music for an imagined life. In those times, a revolution lived in difficult terrain, launching forays into the cities only to confirm the desperation of the populace. Victorious rebellions, whether velvet or sandpaper in character, were but seeds in the soil of mass graves of dissenters. The arts were a lilt and a laugh, government by catharsis. Thus he was at hand when the army was ordered into the streets and, when the tenant across the hall was dragged off by soldiers, he caught the last plane out. How could he, of all people, have been in Cuba, in Serbia, in Nicaragua when the earth shook? He seemed always to be appearing at the edge of some precipice. As when, in a seaside village of southern Spain, the members of the *Guardia Civil*, posted at the corner with Uzis, ran their fingers through his son's hair in delight while the landlady asserted that Franco was already dead but didn't know it. One must acknowledge that native revolutionaries do not commit suicide. It is the soldiers of the invading armies who take their own lives. How had he been an army officer during an improvident war, and the soldiers volunteering for a lost cause? He thinks he betrayed his mind by trying to make other people's sense. Comparisons are odious, and ignorance is bliss.

CM:
From the Vineyard to the Sea

Now he knew that he would be counted among the vinedressers to whom the landowner sent his servants and his son to collect the fruit; if he was not the first one to pick up a stone, and his aim was as wayward as his heart, still he threw it with all his might, with predictable results—a crime translated into parable. Nor was it a complete surprise to learn that he would have followed the crowd to the governor's palace, demanding the release of another prisoner, raising his voice at the approach of the praetorian guards. He would have named names if he had been called to the inquiry (he sometimes wished he had), for he had built his house on a bluff where everything was permitted; its cornerstone was his conviction that he had done nothing wrong, harmed no one very seriously except himself; necessity was the flag he raised on his front lawn. To give up his accountant's peculiar methodology, his brother's escape route, his wife's dark secret—these disclosures were of a piece with his decision to melt down his silverware and hide the bricks in a well: a matter of self-preservation. At dusk he walked along the trail that curved around the bluff, his eyes fixed on the horizon, where a boat with black sails was coming about. He was muttering to himself, making a list of everyone for whom he had done a favor. And all for what?

MB:
Forensics

The apparent objectivity of objects is merely a useful façade, their visibility a deception like that of a citizen planning an escape even as he carries a flag to the obligatory show of support and wears the lapel pin of blanket patriotism. The hidden silverware retains a picture of the one who scratched at the dirt with a fork to bury it before fleeing. The discarded bricks took a handprint with them to the bottom of the well. If one were to reanimate the seemingly lifeless and inert objects around us, one would see how exile, insurgency, paramilitaries, preemption and intervention trouble the mirror and the goblet, how turmoil takes the seabed, and the massed bodies point toward both those accountable and the marked who survived. Were we able to christen the knuckle of a tree or the imprint of a shoe, the vinegar of a dead crow, a slice of bread . . . . I offer these examples only to reveal the enormity of the task. If the chimes were a weather vane, if the arrow were a wing, if the calendar were ancient graffiti . . . . The guilt of the survivor undoes the efficacy of a fallout shelter. To picture a life without friends is to be bereft in advance. The Apocalypse, don't miss it. Count on it. Take it to the bank. All objects are *objets d'arte*.

CM:
Afghanistan

She said that what I saw I did not see: a Predator drone taxiing down the runway of an airbase near the border with Pakistan and taking off toward the mountains. And where I went I did not go: a house in which young women wrote in secret, nibbling tea cookies in a narrow white room that looked out on a snowbound garden. And what I heard I did not hear: a story told by the crippled woman seated by the woodstove, who used both hands to straighten out her legs. *Let's go to school,* her father said when she was little. *School:* a marvelous word for a girl confined to her house. What did I see? An old man rubbing his dislocated shoulder beyond the street of butcher shops. A bomb-sniffing dog biting its trainer's arm. Soviet medals for sale on a table covered with knives. Where did I go? The gym, the canteen, and the *Duck and Cover*—a windowless bar on the other side of the tunnel. What did I hear? The whirr of helicopters, the footsteps of an aid official running on the treadmill, acronyms: PRT, IDP. The armored vehicle that took me to a roundtable discussion was called an MRAP (Mine Resistant Ambush Protected); the soldier swiveling around in the turret, aiming his mounted gun at cars and buildings, couldn't believe the mission was for poetry. The word on everybody's tongue was *kinetic*—i.e., dangerous. I was marking days off the calendar in my hooch when the duck and cover warning sounded. Under the bunk bed I crawled to wait for the all clear signal. What did I see? A photograph of a green-eyed Afghan woman taken before the Russians came. Everybody knows her.

MB:
The Scope

I confess that in any group of three, I am two. Myself watching myself. I admit that, in my writings, the third person, while not me, is someone who knows a lot about me. Thus have I altered the first person pronoun so that he is I and will be I long after the one who here inhabits the I has gone. What am I getting at? It is to suggest that projection and abstraction are ways to transcend the tangible gang war that is contemporary nationalisms. To conjecture that artifice, fancy, illusion, fable and the generalized vision made possible by abstraction are what we use to save ourselves, day after day. We inhabit them. We push ourselves out of ourselves to inhabit them. If there are those who do not buy it, well, they have their own escapes. Some went under the bed, some to the cellar, some to the woods. Some enlisted, some went to prison to be safe. Some sought anonymity—if not off the grid, of a profile so low they would be overlooked by the satellites and could readily stay off the moving target. We were writing students when Dr. Finch, our nervous professor and cellist, praised Lew's story, in which a distraught salesman on the way home stopped in a penny arcade to fire a rifle beam at the midsection of a glassed-in bear. Our beloved teacher noted that the shooter was at the same time shooting his reflection on the glass. The bear reared, growled, and reversed his course with each hit. The man shot himself again and again. For the moment, his truth lay in the efficacy of a rifle scope. I had no symbolism in me and did not understand. Lew's was the best of our stories, because his troubled character would remain in the arcade, never running out of quarters and bullets. He is still there, he will always be there. That was Lew's achievement. Some went under the bed and are still there, some to the woods, some to prison. Some wrote about it.

CM:
Tactics

How we inhabit earth and air, mask and stage, determines what is recorded in the ledger of lost hours: so said the healer who sent us out along the trade routes to spread his teachings, which did not attract as many followers as he had hoped. We were surprised to learn that his ideas derived not from divine revelation but from a reference in a history of sea battles dating to antiquity. That we could not grasp the complexity of his thought was for him a source of mirth until we began to take pride in our ignorance. Then he likened us to acrobats on a farewell tour; issued inscrutable decrees—*If I is another . . . . If I am inscribed in cloud and stone;* upset the delicate balance we had established, at the start of our journey, between the desire to serve some larger purpose and the imperatives of daily life. Our letters requesting clarification went unanswered; also our pleas for money. Years passed. And we had all but forgotten his charge to us when a perfumed envelope was delivered to the youngest member of our troupe, at a feast in a provincial capital which (we feared) we might never leave; the handwriting was unfamiliar, but the phrasing recalled the spell cast one night on the roof of his house in the desert. At last we understood the nature of his deception: the royal messenger who also served as the king's bodyguard, a warrior with a literary turn of mind, was entrusted with the responsibility of defending the nation when its neighbor, blessed with a larger navy and stronger gods, besieged the palace from the sea. *The battle is at its height,* he said after being struck by a stray bullet. *Do not announce my death.* The invaders withdrew within the week. Now we knew what to do.

MB:

Aesthetic Wobble #3

Tricks and maneuvers, stagecraft, gambits and ploys—the journey from mind to mindful to no-mind goes by way of dream and the inexpressible. If you have to fight, say the ninjas, you have lost. We live out a tautology among power surges. Slaves become senators and senators become slaves. Luminaries flash and pass away in the scent of bad wiring. Casualty figures are lowered for the home front and morbidity cut out of the films. The politician bribes others to fight in his place. In the aftermath we hoard the peels of the burnt skin of veterans. In such circumstances, we would surely die from being morose if we lacked the inexpressible. I still like the moon, its icy visage, once the cache of our romance. One can't help but smile at a clown face, a toddler, or a band made up entirely of tubas. No doubt a religious feeling permeates the lunar hoodoos of southern Utah. We try to slow the Sufi, those circling in a Hora, the sprinter, the fast talker, the one jumping to the ferry deck as it starts to leave the pier. We want to approach them palms up in supplication. It has become harder to manage. By now, in the cold or at three a.m., I have to force my fingers to be flat. I had intended to question the guru, but it wasn't yet peacetime. It's just that we know too much of the wrong things. He who thought he could jump onto the ferry as it was leaving wrongly assumed the ferry would be where he landed. We have little capacity for seeing ahead. Lacking communion with the inexpressible, we are hostages to the past. Our favorite stunt is the parade.

CM:
Proverbs

Spring doesn't arrive with a single flower, said the woman in the blue burqa. When I asked for another proverb, she said: *You have to wait your turn even if your father owns the mill.* Nor did the parade turn out the way I thought it would. No one was overcome by tear gas; water cannons were not deployed; the crowd dispersed peacefully, drawn by the music playing in the carousel. Children in the plaza wrote wishes on balloons and released them into the sky, waiting for three men dressed up as kings to arrive on an elephant, a camel, and a donkey. I invented reasons for my failure to see what was plain to everybody else: the scales were unreliable, the police recruits would never pass the exam, bounty hunters outnumbered escaped slaves. But I had misread the story. *Avoid the forest if you're afraid of wolves,* said the woman in the burqa. I said: *Eyes fear, hands do.* There was no bread in the oven, yet I preferred to dwell on the rumor that a one-eyed lion was buried in the stadium. *No family without a black sheep,* I said. *You're a shoemaker without shoes,* she said. Field Day was what I remembered: how the near-sighted boy was favored to win the fifty-yard dash; how the neighbor's pet crow landed on his shoulder as he ran; how he stopped just short of the finish line. That boy was me.

MB:

Aesthetic Wobble #4

I have been enamored of the eternality of the proverb and the koan, as I have been susceptible to the present tense of the Existential. I do not know if each such preoccupation was a negotiation with, a concession to, or an escape from the sociopolitical. I, like others, have time and again written the carnage. It may be a kind of reasoning to say that art imitates nature, but we are burdened with the question as to what is reasonable. We know that literature is an extraction, by turns opalescent or silvery, leaden or toxic. We mine the dark. We scrape with our eyes equally the petroglyphs of Anasazi ruins and the inscriptions of the Mayans. We seek in excess and deprivation the nature of a soul. We learn that every moment is one of suspension between this and that. We have tests and proverbs: *Dumplings in a dream are not dumplings, but a dream; If a horse had anything to say, he would speak up; Sleep faster, we need the pillows.* You and I, Reader, are privy, not to time, but to entropy. We are the Gurdjieff-Ouspensky devotee, the one who reminds us that being fully awake is possible only for a minute or two at a time, and who takes us up in his two-seater and stalls the engine. Here, he said, I'll show you. I am here today to say that he got the plane started again.

CM:
A Note on Aesthetics

Like coins, proverbs circulate, burnished by contact with others, weighed and judged, their value rising or falling according to forces beyond the control of any individual—geography, weather, the price of grain, war, plague, changing tastes. To the supply of minerals add the demands of the imagination, which can summon into being a social order capable of buttressing or overturning belief. *To your health!* The sommelier toasted his last customers, a banker who was explaining to a fashion model why the currency of the age, invention, resembled less a silver ingot than a wave in the sea, ebbing and flooding. (His business card read: *Wisdom is better than precious stones.*) Better to be liquid than subject to, he liked to say. And: *a dog has four legs, but only goes one way.* What did she think? *From the mouths of old men comes bad breath and wisdom.* From her necklace hung a coin, minted in Constantinople for the Council of Nicaea, where the emperor ordered the bishops to compose a creed, which would survive floods, and famine, and the fall of Rome. To pay his soldiers, said the banker, one emperor melted down statues for coins, and still there was unrest, which left the city unprepared for the final assault. He leaned over the table to examine the coin, which he would not say was real until the sommelier had gone. The model held her breath. Yes, it was just the right accent for her dress.

MB:
On Time

First cosmology charmed, then captured, the physicists, who twisted and turned in the galactic wind, squinting to chart the constant speed of light through time in search of the irrefutable. Unable to approach from beforehand the Big Bang, they had to embrace the "Inflationary" Big Bang, theorizing, from a minuscule extract, the birth of a universe. They speculated on when time began and why time speeds up or drags. I know only that endorphins can hurry us, even while our electrochemical self has long since slowed. Hence, worldly time takes the measure of entropy, for which each of us is another proof. If civilization has been a holding action against doom, that knowledge has been neither prescient nor counsel. Would we be running in place if we believed in time? It was because the conquerors could do no better than the embedded gods of nature, to which the native peoples gave obeisance, that it was decided to conscript the local culture into the church of the captors. A culture of centuries, erased in a flash. The origin of the universe will be traced in equations because words cannot reach back to where there was nothing, save they alchemize. Poetry is born in the absence of the possibility of poetry. Time or entropy? History bleeds time all the way back to zilch. The famed Red Sox hitter, Ted Williams, had superior eyes. The more one sees, the slower the pitch. This end time is endless.

CM:
Holding Action

They knew he was no longer listening—and still they pleaded with him, one after another, on the conference call arranged by the therapist, to remember what he loved: the fragrance of sagebrush after rain; the taste of red chili stew on an autumn afternoon; the entrance of the chorus in Beethoven's last symphony; the way the wounded raptors at the rehabilitation center perched on his forearm; the connections that he made between the healing and creative arts. What equation can explain the desire for self-destruction? Late into the night they argued with him, invoking the history of artistic reinvention, the secrets of cosmology, debts owed to the living. He asked them not to blame his wife. The next time he would take no chances. Their alchemy was humor—useless on a man who does not want to live. *It's sad, but it's funny,* was what he planned to have inscribed on his gravestone before he lost his way. His final instructions were unambiguous: *Mix my ashes with all the animals that have gone before me into the darkness.* The therapist praised his honesty; his friends wished him well; the call came to an end. No one was surprised the night the K9 unit found him lying behind his house, with a bullet in his head, barely breathing. For three days, the nurses in the ICU monitored his vital signs, playing his favorite recording of the *Ninth Symphony,* the chorus always entering on cue, open unto eternity.

MB:
The Revolution Needs a Song

When events occur for which there are only insufficient words, when movement is forbidden, when there is only an odor of ash in darkness, when every sense has been stifled, when we wake in chains, there remains a simmering of song, a residue in which a microscopic ferment has already begun. Take two chopsticks on a countertop, a comb between two scraps of paper, two spoons to slap against a knee, a length of vinyl hose into which one has wedged a mouthpiece. If it causes you to sing or dance, if it pumps your heart or fills your lungs or rattles your spine, then you are, for the nonce, in the realm of the infinite no-mind, carried by a progression of changes. Now anything can happen. Never mind the key sign, the metronome, the trumpet players counting rests while the strings fill the hall. Never mind the danger to the longtime oboist, the bruised lips of the brass players, the stiffening fingers of the pianists. Forget that the players make music at a high personal cost. That's the profession. I am speaking here of the nature of rhythm, pitch, melody, phrasing and harmony. The five food groups of the soul. Take a tingly triangle, a horsey woodblock, bowls full of tympani, the simplicity of a pipe with valves, the sonorous metalwork of a steel drum, a fretless washtub bass. The barest rhythm or tune can imprison or free us, and the words of songs, like dreams, are incontestable. Music always wins.

CM:
Tamara Khanum (1906-1991)

"A strange feeling has come over me," said my interpreter. I didn't realize until he looked down at his feet that he was speaking for himself, not the museum guide, whose enthusiastic summary of the Armenian dancer's life included the detail that women from her village were stoned to death, by their brothers or husbands, after following her advice to remove their veils. "Somehow I know," he explained, "that if I lived at that time I would have tortured my sister to death." He was an excellent translator, accustomed to working with military delegations, and it seemed to me that he chose the word *tortured* deliberately, his professionalism overriding his reservations about the wisdom of revealing such a thought. The tour concluded in the unheated display room with a video of Khanum performing first for workers digging a canal in the Fergana Valley and then for rapt audiences across the Soviet Union. In the glass cases were dresses from Norway and Latvia, China and Kazakhstan: scores of lands whose dances and songs she mastered and improvised on. The interpreter, watching her step lightly across a stage in a kimono, remarked that in her lifetime Uzbeks considered her to be—what was the term? *Persona non grata.* Now she was a national symbol. There was a story about the dress from Belarus: how government officials visiting from Minsk, after the war, wept at the sight of it, the Nazis having eradicated much of their culture; from its pattern of blue and red, and the dance she performed for them, the marriage of music and movement she enacted on this wooden floor, twirling like their women, singing in their language with a native accent, they discovered how to revive their traditions. It didn't matter to me if the story was true.

MB:
Jack

Given an invitation to an audience with the Pope, the gift of a diplo-
mat who had taken a fancy to the young couple shipboard on their
honeymoon, Jack worried about protocol, he being a non-Catholic.
Standing apart, barely inside the door through which His Eminence
would enter, aware that he was among the faithful, he reminded him-
self not to be caught up in the drama. Finally, a gong sounded, the
door flew open, and, sure enough, Jack fell to his knees and kissed
the Pope's ring. Every such story has an aftermath subject to entropy.
This otherwise dramatic and amusing anecdote must needs be dull
to one impervious to the vibration of a gong, the suddenness of the
hush that must have overtaken the chamber at the sound of said
gong, and the splashiness of the Pope's vestments as he parted the
sea of sinners. Imagine the buzz, the urgent quiet, and then the visual
riot that so far exceeded Jack's expectation. We shall, shall we not,
forsooth kneel in space, as we must fall, again and again, for those
artists who proclaim the ecstatic body in its local wrap. All cultures
venerate the power of the sensate and the imaginative, interlaced in
what we know as beauty, to separate us from that portion of the
life force that fights for survival. An uprising will have a marching
song the occupiers mistake for an agreeable air, and a dance they
take for gaiety as it gradually surrounds them.

CM:
The List

After the uprising, he learned that his name was on a list of people
to be arrested and shot on the anniversary of Gaddafi's bloodless
coup. The colonel had once executed twelve hundred political pris-
oners on a single day—a fraction of what was planned to celebrate
his long reign and warn off the insurgents approaching Tripoli. For-
tunately, the regime fell a week before the massacre could be carried
out, and now my friend was showing Free Libya to poets visiting
from abroad. Here were the ruins of the dictator's compound, here
was a seaside hotel commandeered by the transitional government,
and here was a road through a barren valley where battles had raged
only months before. I picked up a bullet casing, as a keepsake. My
friend didn't want to know which of his neighbors had put his name
on the list (he was one of sixty targeted in his village), preferring to
discuss his plans for another poetry festival. On we drove to Yefren,
in the Western Mountains, where Gaddafi's son was being held for
trial. Painted on the walls was the Berber flag—bands of blue to
symbolize the sea, green for the mountains, and yellow for the
desert, through which ran in red, for resistance and freedom, the last
letter of the alphabet: two crescent moons lying back to back, con-
nected by a line. On a ridge above more ruins my friend insisted
that the dictator's son would be treated well until he was hanged.
Then he clapped his hands to usher us back into the vans. He had
a list of things for us to see before it grew dark.

MB:

Aesthetic Wobble #5

When are we used up? If we live in the interstices of conflict enlarged by weaponry, and we do, if we calculate with zeros, and we do, if we are moving inexorably to a robotic ideal of paradise, and we are, I must still teach my children how to protect their hearts without stilling them. This may be increasingly the function of art: not to distract us from fire and brimstone but to laugh at hubris and love the miniscule. Beyond space and the depth of oceans lies the true final frontier, human frailty, which science seeks to overcome through biochemical manipulation. And what would be the province of art without the corrupt and vacuous? Where lies bliss if not in the concept of the blessing? What blessing in paradise? Aristotle was right: art without bloodletting is an insufficient salve.

CM:
Angkor

What I heard in the temple—the whine of cicadas at dusk, the voices of my friends taking in the profiles of the Buddha chiseled in the stone towers, the guide's silence before he explained that the figures in one bas-relief were not fishermen asleep in a boat but soldiers slain in battle—must have been shaped by what I saw at the genocide museum—barbed wire; a bloodstained bed and chamber pot; a rack of iron shackles; instruments of torture; the photographs of the condemned; a sign forbidding laughter. *Do you know*—this was the refrain of the crone who escorted us from the gallows to the high school classrooms in which thousands of "traitors" were confined before being sent to the killing fields near Phnom Penh. Torture was the theme of the paintings on the walls, executed by one of the seven survivors of the camp; in a documentary film available in the local market (among pirated copies of *Modern Family*) the artist confronted his former guards and torturers, who to his dismay called themselves the chief victims of the Khmer Rouge. *I lock the door,* one said over and over, replaying his nightly duties with relish. *Do you know,* said the crone, *in the end they turned on one another.* Lightning flashed above the trees, temples, and floating villages in Angkor. Mosquitoes buzzed around us (it was dengue season, blood donors were needed at the children's hospital), and when I told the guide that we had seen enough he flashed a smile. The embassy had recommended him—his clients included Bill Clinton—and we were grateful for his sense of humor. Earlier in the day, he had pointed at the roots of a banyan tree curled over a wall until we finally got the joke: did it look as if he was sticking his finger in someone's ass? Yes, it did. *Funny, isn't it?* he said. *Your president liked that.*

MB:
Thermal

It was in the days when cruelty still wore a disguise that a nation hung by its radios to learn if the child who had fallen into the well would be pulled to safety. It was in a time when the national cemeteries had more space than they would ever need that the order came down to assemble for yearly training in chemical-biological-radiological weaponry, against which we were to use masks, special injections and cowardice or fatalism—take your choice. The military thought education was the cat's meow, while the academy considered the military to be mad dogs. Each time we went to war, the generals disagreed behind closed doors. It was in a time when the term "friendly fire" had little use and still held its irony, and when captains of industry were in plain sight, that many enlisted with an eye toward a skill to be used in civilian life. The front lines were to be their safety nets. It was back in the age of selective memory, when the aftermath of military service was heroic, sometimes humorous, absurdist with a smile, that Major Yoshikatsu Yatsunami, about to speak of Japan to an audience of American officers, leapt from the stage wearing a Kabuki outfit to taunt the colonel. It was before we knew that everything happens at once. So it was in the Age of Chivalry that the perfected catapult changed warfare. Ideas were the casualties of combat. Abstract thinking dies in the heat of battle and reporters paint the news red. The first principle of war is that every weapon will be used.

CM:
Utopia

A waitress in the fish market, in Maputo, tugged me toward a picnic table, a fierce look in her eyes, twisting my hand until something popped in my wrist. Our contact from the embassy hailed us from a table in the back, and as we pushed past the hawkers of cashews, miniature bicycles made of wire, and sarongs I wondered if I had broken a bone. We had just come from viewing a new bronze statue, cast in North Korea, of Samora Machel, whose vow to build a socialist paradise in Mozambique had led to civil war. The founding president stood with his right hand raised, as if to explain to the invisible masses why they should drive their colonial masters back to Portugal and their African enemies into the sea. A million people died to usher in a new regional order. One idea gives way to another at the barrel of a gun. (Emblazoned on the flag was an AK-47.) Machel died in a plane crash, Marxism was abandoned, and now the future was said to be bright: natural gas fields had been discovered, the Chinese were building a new airport . . . . Emblems of the old order remained. The American Center stood on the corner of Mao Tse Tung Avenue and Kim Il Sung. (Our program was poorly attended.) On one wall of the French Cultural Center was a work titled *Utopia*, by a Zimbabwean artist in exile: two charred pages framing a book wired shut, in a cage hung from a sheet of rusted metal on which were inscribed words like *history* and *night* . . . . For lunch we were served shrimp and crab, kingfish and calamari, clams and rice. Ravenous, I rubbed my swelling wrist, and asked for more.

MB:
Bled

I go back to 1983. At the P.E.N. conference in Bled, a war story novelist had risen to say that Tito had assured him that anything could be put into a novel because, as Tito had put it, "Everything happens." Yet the learned theoreticians and critics, men and women of exquisite vocabularies, who had been laboring to make sense of nuance, hint, disjunction, fragmentation and the most elaborate and trendy of tangential approaches, had said nothing of the recently imprisoned poet, causing the veteran novelist to rise again to suggest in frustration that the theme of the next conference should be, "Writers Against Writers." It happened before tribal voting blocs carried elections, and dissolution became a tactic the world over. At our television taping, the Russian poet had worn his war medals on his leather jacket. Wherever we were taken, we were shown the town memorial to the Jews, then taken for drinks with the mayor. Into this make-work schedule the Russian inserted a poem for each occasion, written on the bus ride. He knew, as we said, which side his bread was buttered on. It comes down to a personal decision: will one join up or not, and can one survive otherwise? Fathers and mothers who left a motherland or fatherland were prescient or lucky. Every event is an omen in retrospect. Say what we will, everything happens.

2

Postcripts

MB:
Meteor

February 15, 2013, Chelyabinsk, Russia, offers us the chance for an afterword to the white shock of a meteor that stoked the bitter embers of resignation. Oh, we had long thought the sky was falling when it was only starting to. The wind has carried Chicken Little to the far reaches of our imagining. Turmoil blocks the exits. Indoor videos show workers querulous between stopping in their tracks and ducking beneath a desk. A sunrise seven-ton fireball. A shock wave twenty times Hiroshima's. An aftermath. They could hide but they couldn't run. That's the never-ending story after a piece of sky falls, empowering those who now have new words for the future as it ripples through time and space. It's the work of cheerful doomsayers to empty the stone of its weight. It' a task behind rose-tinted glasses to see despair in the tea leaves. Only a depression? you ask. Did you mean a universal melancholia or merely a concave work of art? Portents of last feelings fall to earth as artillery, space junk and star chips, to be mistaken for instructions. In the aftermath of the meteor, the telescopes crane their necks to see if it is time. In Chelyabinsk, cars go faster to gobble up the future in dashboard cams. Now it can be told that the meteor briefly outshone the sun.

CM:
Brown vs. Board of Education

20 February 2013. Washington, D.C. The associate justice described for the dinner guests the lag time between the Supreme Court decision and its implementation: how Eisenhower dismissed the warning that he would have to reoccupy the entire South if he sent troops to Little Rock; how he chose the fabled 101st Airborne to escort nine black children past the protesters; how brave the children were. The governor closed the schools the next year, and the battle continued. *Finish it*, demanded the Freedom Rider in the film excerpt shown during dessert. In the matter of the people versus the advancement of civil rights, how do you find? We cling to what we know—and then the intersection lights up, blinding everyone: drivers and passengers, policemen, the road crew. The meteor streaking across the sky was long past before the sound waves arrived, injuring hundreds of people drawn to the windows to see the light. Shards of glass everywhere. No telling how long it will take for the wounds to heal and the damage to be repaired.

MB:
Relativity

Publication of "The General Theory of Relativity," Albert Einstein, 1916. There was some applause, followed by rugged treks with elephantine telescopes seeking an eclipse. The proof was in the sky. Spring forward: Terry, our friend, expert in radiation shielding, is telling of a couple who were taken aboard a spaceship. We are not laughing. The proof is in the sky. Spring forward: quantum physics in the church means God may think he has given us free will, but is changing the experiment by his presence. Spring forward: an unidentified future will be bent by gravitation and desire. Of my education, I remember what I want to: Ashley Montague has come to another campus to speak on "The Natural Superiority of Women." I have permission to skip ethics class if I agree to report on it. After the talk of chromosomes, he speaks also of polar people who recognize no up or down, no left or right. Spring forward: General Eisenhower leaves the presidency, warning against becoming a warfare nation, and today a statue of the genius of relativity sits in the side yard of the Academy of Sciences at peace, a twelve-foot, rumpled, kindly old fellow, the universe spread out before him, where children who have no need of the universal climb into his lap just because he looks okay. Because of Einstein, it is not too late. Absent Einstein, if you are living in the past, you are out of time.

CM:
Radioactivity

Posthumous publication of *Radioactivity*, Marie Curie, 1935. She was reluctant to leave off work to deliver a Nobel lecture on noticing how isolated isotopes glowed with a light, which I sometimes imagine seeing in my hands after the incident in the VA hospital. Sylvia and I were driving west, two student athletes devoted to pleasure, and when we stopped in Chicago to visit Toby we thought: sex, tennis, cocaine, Heineken. But Toby needed my help dismantling an X-ray room at the VA, and for three days we smashed walls with sledgehammers, pried the table off its foundation, took turns battering the radioactive shield. We were like wild men until he cut the wire anchoring the X-ray machine to the ceiling, and it sliced through my fingertip. I left a trail of blood following my friend to the emergency room, and when they refused to treat me (I wasn't a veteran) Toby barged into the office and ordered the doctor to stitch my finger back together. He spoke with such authority that no one contradicted him. Sylvia and I continued west the next day, my finger throbbing; she waited until after we had graduated to hook up with my friend; they're still married. Sometimes I sweat when I write, which I attribute to what I absorbed in the X-ray room. Curie's curiosity earned her two Nobel Prizes and an early death from blood cancer. I earned enough money at the VA to make it to Berkeley, where Sylvia and I liked to do lines of coke before we hit the courts. Her backhand was a thing of beauty.

MB:
Clive Wearing, March, 1985

There can be no postscripts in the consciousness of Mr. Wearing, whose brain's mechanisms for saving and retrieving short-term memories were eradicated by encephalitis. Wrapped in both anterograde and retrograde amnesia, for decades he recorded in a journal, sometimes minute by minute, the exact time, with the notation that he was now awake, now "really, completely" awake, now "perfectly, overwhelmingly" awake . . . . Always, he has greeted his wife passionately, as if for the first time, which to him it always is. His condition confirms our fragile dependence on story, and on the artifice of the linear. I think we cannot help but ruminate "after the fact," a life thus defined as much by the past as by visible scarring, blemishes and disfigurement—all the symptoms of a carcass-in-waiting. It is a truism that the truth will set you free, but not that it will make you happy, except it free you from the vain struggle not to surrender. I was crossing the street when I met S. midway and asked how she was. "Oh," she said, wearily, "my life is all orgasm and repose," and we hurried off in opposite directions. A week later, meeting again between the lines of traffic, asked how she was, S. said, "I don't know if I want to know the truth or be loved." Mr. Wearing cannot remember his immediate past. We had best reconsider, who wish to live "in the moment." Memory was never a matter of time, but of entropy. I know this from looking back.

CM:
Hiatus

As I Lay Dying, William Faulkner, 1930. The scorpion skittered between my friend's salad plate and my silverware, dropped over the edge of the table set up on the beach, and disappeared. At the Hyatt on Saadiyat Island in Abu Dhabi we were celebrating the completion of a diplomatic mission and my friend's birthday: white wine and dates, salt wind and the sound of the surf. In the blank space behind us rose the unfinished buildings—villas, museums, a university—of the new cultural center designed by architects from around the world. In the morning I would leave for Baghdad, on another mission, which might be scuttled by the sectarian violence marking the anniversary of Saddam Hussein's birthday. I was rereading Faulkner in preparation for a class at the embassy, struck this time by the image of Jewell calming a horse risen up on its hindquarters. "They stand in a rigid terrific hiatus," the horse and the young man, which might describe my situation. For your name was inscribed inside the front cover of my copy; dozens of passages were underlined in the first third of the novel; apparently you didn't finish it. Nor could I discern a pattern in what caught your attention. And your last high-lighted sentence—*"I'm bounding toward God and my reward, Cora sung"*—inspired less than brilliant marginalia: *Cora-religious, the fish*. I recalled you licking a spoon dripping with chocolate fondue; how you left me in spirit long before our formal break; a venomous poem that I dedicated to you. There comes a moment in the novel when Jewell climbs up on the horse to ride to the barn, saying, "You can quit now, if you got a plenty"—which is what I dreamed of finding with you, in the unreconstructed South of the imagination, where the novelist knew the war would never end.

MB:
V

July 19, 1941. Prime Minister Winston Churchill begins to use the V
hand sign. The Nazis have the Swastika, but the Allies would have
the wishbone, as well as thumbs-up, the okay signal, and the one-
finger rigid digit salute. I'd sit on a carton of goods for the five-and-
ten and write down on the cardboard the casualty reports from the
radio. I'd report the numbers to my father when he came home from
the store. Few now take note of it being the war that followed the
War-To-End-All-Wars. Upbeat was in. We defied local authority,
in a random gesture of free speech. Giving the finger from afar
would be lost in the distance so we adjusted, raising a fist and, with
the other hand, slapping the bicep. A gesture known elsewhere as
the *bras d'honneur* and the Iberian slap. On us, it looked natural, as
the watch fob, bow tie, cigar, Homburg and eloquence fit the Prime
Minister. In retrospect, how far we were from those events of which
we felt a part. It was a time when immigrants like my father severed
their histories so as to Americanize their children. The war was far.
Language was wobbling to accommodate the war effort. By the time
Richard Nixon flashed the V to signal victory in Vietnam, victory
meant defeat, and the V of two fingers had become a sad, ironic
protestation shortly to be made quaint in a digital age.

CM:
Haze

The Man Who Planted Trees, Jean Giono, 1954. Suppose the assignment
is to write a story that will change the world. Begin with a memo-
rable character—a shepherd will do—who lives alone (say he lost
his family) and can thus conduct his mission without attracting at-
tention. To restore a ruined valley he will plant a hundred acorns
every day for more than thirty years, in snow and rain, in sickness
and war, venturing ever farther from his sheepfold. Hunters are the
first to notice the change in the landscape, though they cannot name
it, and by the time the government grasps the import of his secret
project the shepherd has sympathizers in the region and the capital
who are captivated by the shade, the wildlife, the torrent of water
surfacing from underground streams. Young couples move into the
valley to renovate houses, a road is built, life returns. The shepherd's
story charms readers, and as it is translated into other languages
communities around the world adopt tree-planting policies to shade
their streets and stave off the effects of climate change. One day on
a driving tour of western China, near the source of the Yellow River,
I count the seedlings planted in straight lines on a hillside, recalling
my walk in the heat and haze of Beijing, where pollution from cars
and coal-fired power plants had blocked the sun for weeks. I could
barely breathe that day. *Too little, too late*, I think, as the van rushes on.

MB:
Kitty Hawk

North Carolina, December 17, 1903, 10:35 a.m. First came the mytho-
logical: airborne gods, a winged father and son, the poets' flying
horse. Set in narratives, read into belief, construed to be the
metaphors of seers, time extended the story. In Kitty Hawk would
be sketched the first tentative shape of infinity. Wilbur and Orville's
glider trials paid homage to wind—a hop and a skip. If manned
flight brought forth strafing and bombing, the delivery cross-oceans
of exotic diseases, the exporting of inflation to nations in the time-
less zones of the undeveloped—such was the cost in the new para-
digm for a limitless future. If one were unable to climb the rungs
of social class, one might at least mount the sky. That would perhaps
be sufficient for the short run, the thrill of the means: the taxi and
liftoff, the panorama of billowy clouds beneath one's wings, the tilt
toward an extended sunset, the invisible corridors to anywhere. For
it was elsewhere where both infinity and eternity lay—if not past
the horizon, surely in the suborbital, on the far side of the moon,
past the nearest stars, beyond our solar system. We looked to pilots
to spot those extraterrestrials we thought distant cousins come to
make known the reach of our extended family. They would be . . .
not rivals, but paragons of loyalty, watching over a planetary hospice
from a height that requires clean oxygen. However long the argu-
ments might last, if we plant enough trees there may occur over time
the exponential benefit of proof.

CM:
Petty

Sky Above Clouds IV, Georgia O'Keeffe, 1965. Rows of white ellipses arranged like icebergs on a blue sea, with a pink ribbon on the horizon. "What one sees from the air," the painter wrote, "is so simple and so beautiful I cannot help feeling that it would do something wonderful for the human race—rid it of much smallness and pettishness if more people flew." If I had opened the door to the courtyard. If I had waited longer in the café. If I had ridden the horse fated to throw her over the fence . . . The gate agent was beckoning to the last passenger in the waiting area, who could not bring himself to say goodbye to a woman in a yellow dress. She had surprised him by the monitor displaying flight information—his was delayed by a thunderstorm—and when she suggested coffee he smiled for the first time in days. He had loved her long ago, in another city, and as they traded stories about their work and families he tried to recall his reasons for breaking off their affair. Likely they were small. *Petty* was the word she used to describe the owner of the gallery where her drawings were sold. Perhaps she applied it to him as well. The agent walked over to say that the gate was closing. He started to rise. "Don't worry," the artist told him, reaching for his hand. "They always hold the plane for lovers."

MB:

Nu descendant un escalier n° 2, 1912

Marcel Duchamp was not, one hazards, without guile in naming his canvas. Let the metal cones and cylinders glitter in the mind, free of such fabrics as would reshape the light. *Nature morte* lives! It must have appeared to critics to be the Nubile Descent of a Cyborg. I smile, I laugh, I bow to the art history that so imbued the nude with its nakedness that flesh ranked above sinew and bone. Duchamp's nude inflamed the keepers of still lives, with its suspended motion, its skeletal jibe at the tedium of titillation, its jangling expectation. In 1878, Eadweard Muybridge's sequential photographs of "Sallie Gardner at a Gallop," had proved that a galloping horse lifts all four legs at once. His twenty-four images of motionless motion, superimposed, may be imagined a precursor to Duchamp's "Nude." In a universe of entropy, bone prevails. I remember the twenty-fifth mile of the marathon. My foolhardy, amateur run up Diamond Head was difficult, in that climbing taxes the lungs, but the descent after twenty-four miles was the pain of bone on bone. Why do we do these things? Context means that each act is a comment upon its predecessors, and every painting has a kissing cousin. The student potter was told by her teacher, "If you have any attachment to your pot, you had better break it right now." Duchamp: "I don't believe in art. I believe in artists."

CM:
The Names

Ten Thousand Lives, Ko Un, 1986. An assistant stacked his collected works, a hundred and fifty volumes and counting, on the lower shelves of his new bookcase, anchoring the mountain studio built for him by the city. Outside on the tables were slices of pears and pots of tea; soundlessly a plane crossed the sky. *Numbers have viruses,* said the poet, who decided in solitary confinement to memorialize every person he had ever met—a project that brought to mind Czeslaw Milosz's dream, in old age, of writing miniature biographies of everyone he knew. Impossible, of course. But Ko Un possessed the energy of someone half his age. Later in the day, in the parking lot at the fortress in Suwon, when he took my hand and strode with me toward the train, I imagined that in this act of friendship he was also taking my measure, discerning my strengths and weaknesses with the characteristic generosity of his Zen poems. *Wow,* he tells a shooting star. *You recognized me.* Some younger Korean poets dismissed him for what they regarded as his jockeying for the Nobel Prize. The same held for certain Polish poets laboring after Milosz: how to see for oneself in the shade of a great tree? Ko Un did not let go of my hand until we had walked a great distance. Then he clasped his hands together and smiled at me for a while, as if to fix my features in his memory. We boarded the train, which wound around the fortress rebuilt by the last dictator, who had imprisoned and tortured the poet. In the sunlight Ko Un gazed at the walls before writing some lines in his notebook. The train stopped at the archery range, where we took up bows and waited for the order to fire. Ko Un was all skin and bones, yet his hand did not shake when he pulled the arrow back to his chin and aimed at the rings on the target. The trick, I learned, is to aim downward and a little to the left so that the arrow rises to its mark. My father would go through the names of everyone in our family, including pets, before he found the right one. Alas, I inherited this trait—unlike the monk-turned-poet who in his cell vowed not to forget anyone, leaving his mark on the ravaged world. Perhaps he is writing now.

MB:
Brain

January, 1986, Pakistani brothers Basit Farooq Alvi and Amjad Fa-
rooq Alvi release the first computer virus, and we're off and running
in the search for metaphors to characterize the impending digital
deluge. "Brain" is coded to defeat illicit copying of software to
"floppy disks," terminology that suggests the ductility of young
minds. Brain will be followed by Creeper, Concept, Simile and
Mylife, infectious names that suggest, respectively, the years of slow
change, the elbows of polemics, the age of comparisons and an in-
terminable era of confessions. Think of a philosophy movement
named for Arf-Arf, an early Trojan Horse. We could ride that con-
tradiction into the absurdist core of random causation. If it became
an enigma to be theorized, peeled, divvied up and finally emptied
onto the subbasement shelves of stone libraries, it goes to show the
illusions of control by which our brains have parsed the unitary
meter of the cosmos. This morning my coffee pals were torching
the titles of military offensives. They spoke of Operation Just Cause,
of Desert Shield and Desert Storm, but had not heard of Operation
Falconer, Operation Planet X or Operation Ivy Needle. The brain
trusts behind warfare speak a hush-hush language. It will take more
than software to expunge euphemism, obliterate deniability and re-
place declarations of "collateral damage" with the names. Arf-Arf!
Having witnessed the upshot of endless war in our time, we hold
out hope for some straight talk afterward.

CM:
The Hat

Ohio Impromptu, Samuel Beckett, 1981. *Little is left to tell* . . . So begins the play commissioned for an international symposium at Ohio State to mark Beckett's seventy-fifth birthday. He made at least two false starts before completing the short text, which consists of a Reader telling a Listener about the visits of a stranger sent by a former love to comfort him—the dear name that Beckett later admitted belonged to his wife, Suzanne. The men wear long black coats, and from time to time the Listener raps the table, either to have the Reader repeat a phrase or to signal him to continue. The props are simple: a plain white deal table, two armless chairs, an old world Latin Quarter hat similar to the one worn by James Joyce. For our performance, in a little theater on the fifth floor of a walk-up in Soho, the director added a candle. He was late to our rehearsal, having left the hat in his hotel room, so I waited in my long black coat, remembering a certain night. The theater seated thirty, and in the silences between phrases I heard someone's stomach growl, grunts of approval, parrots twittering in the children's room. The Listener was a composer whose knocking had a distinctly musical feel. I closed the book, the sad tale told a final time, and after another knock we waited five beats before laying our hands on the table to stare at each other for twenty seconds or more. The candle was snuffed out, and we kept staring in the darkness. I caught your eye in the talk-back. When asked if I had deliberately mispronounced the word, *unfamiliarity,* I blamed it on the wine. But I was thinking of you. Our second time through the play was so much sadder. *Heartbreaking*, someone said. *Nothing is left to tell*, I repeated before walking out into the night, hatless and giddy.

MB:
The Performance

February 2, 1954. Clarence "Bevo" Francis, playing for Rio Grande College versus Hillsdale College, scores one hundred and thirteen points on thirty-eight field goals and thirty-seven free throws. They said you could see his ribcage from the balcony. Bevo, who may have put up the first jump shot, and who in an earlier contest had scored an unrecognized one hundred and sixteen, was the basketball Believe-It-Or-Not of his time. Nonetheless, it was still a game to Bevo, who refused a National Basketball Association contract and went home to the steel mill and the tire company. People do sometimes turn their backs on celebrity. It's a kind of frugality, a financial plan for the spirit. Oh, but it's hard to let go. They chopped off the head of Ted Williams and froze it for later. They put an asterisk next to Roger Maris' season home run record. They replay every astonishing end zone completion. Then the endless summaries of who won what and who fell flat, and the polls of who do you like, lose their currency at year's end when the faces of the year's famous deaths flicker past. Glory is fleeting, but its effects are forever. Like gods overworked by the scrapes and disasters of human beings, our sports pros play hurt. Later, they may labor to move about and strain to remember. Bevo didn't expect the steel mill to close nor his one-game high to stand for six decades. When the mill shut down, he hunted and fished for food until a job came through. Bevo had a shot at the big time but left the money on the table. He remains the king of the corkscrew jumper.

CM:
Critical Point

9 February 2014. Noriaki Kasai glides downhill in Sochi with his arms by his sides, compressing himself into the curve just before he takes off on his soft skis, soars in a V through the night sky, fixing his gaze beyond where he will land so that he resembles a wing in flight, floating the length of a football field toward the critical point, which bisects the steepest part of the hill, and then touches down in Telemark position just shy of the purple line. This is his seventh Winter Olympics, and though he will not medal in this event he has earned a place in history, jumping more times than anyone else in a sport that does not reward longevity. The oldest winner on the World Cup circuit took no training jumps before the competition began—his latest adaptation to the demands of age; he is said to be looking forward to the Winter Games in South Korea. I am remembering my daughter's decision to abandon her dream of skating in the Olympics in order, as she said, to get a life: another critical point, which I might have recognized if I had not been looking beyond her, toward the future in which her friend, and rival, has just skated her way onto the podium. The pang I felt then was connected to gravity. And now? I am flying.

MB:
White Lines

Roadway lanes marked, 1911. I learned to drive on three-lane "kamikaze" highways. There were frequent head-ons as drivers pulled out to pass in opposite directions and, seeing cars oncoming, decided to gun it. There was no space left in which to pull back in, or perhaps they thought they would make it ahead in time. A critical juncture, a decision that cannot be undone, a point of no return . . . . Time is elastic. It stretches but it also snaps back. Head-ons usually included several passengers. Driving on my island, we learned also to motor in a seaside fog by keeping close to the only thing visible: the white line. It was Edward N. Hines of the Wayne County, Michigan, Road Commission who in 1911 first thought it a good idea to line the lanes. Mr. Hines had seen a milk truck dripping onto the roadway and, if you will forgive me an exhilaration, *wila!* Thus, Trenton's River Road got the first white line. Whatever the referent of "it," someone has to have thought of it first. Who first imagined that a man on skis could launch himself from a high take-off ramp and land alive? Who put an eraser on a pencil? Who thought up maps and drew the lines? Oh, the consequences foreseen and unseen whenever someone thinks up a new "it." The jazz singer who sang in English and French ended her life by leaping from a Manhattan skyscraper. She knew the finality ahead as the ski jumper knows only the end of the runway.

CM:
Heat Lightning

Night Music I, by Dennis Milne. 1988. *Up your kilt, laddie,* was the Scots-
man's favorite toast. It was the time of the Harmonic Convergence,
an astrological alignment said to usher in a period of peace—a good
name, I joked, for his new ensemble, Serenata of Santa Fe, for which
he was composing chamber music. Tired of orchestral life in Lon-
don, the double bassist had moved his family to the high desert,
where he was building a house on forty acres of land near Madrid
(pronounced with the accent on the first syllable). Syncretism was
all the rage; also phrenology, aromatherapy, and crystals, the healing
properties of which remained in dispute; more than one of our ac-
quaintances claimed to have been abducted by aliens. So when my
friend veered across the road one night and plowed into a van, killing
himself and maiming another family, his wife consulted a medium,
who channeled his voice saying that he had gotten distracted by the
beauty of the heat lightning. The state toxicologist took another
view of the matter, which figured into the lawsuit filed by the vic-
tims of the accident. It took me hours to track down a recording
of the first of his nocturnes, performed by a classical guitarist who
later took his life, and what I hear in his dissonant chords is a con-
vergence of forces that came to nothing. When I left New Mexico
to cover the wars in the former Yugoslavia, I sometimes wondered
if my friend was listening that night for a sound that dissipated be-
fore it reached his ears. Or perhaps he was just drunk after working
all day in the sun to lay the foundation for his house. Once I toasted
him at a Robert Burns celebration, and on the drive home I caught
the attention of a policeman, who flashed his lights warning me to
slow down. How I loved my friend's brogue.

MB:
The Act

San Francisco, December 23, 1953. First appearance at the hungry i by comedian Mort Sahl. The "*i*" stood, semi-officially, for the id of the psyche, and perhaps, in its lower case modesty, for the humility of the personal. Was it not also a surrealist pun, a smidgen of Dali from a time when it was fun to befuddle the squares? Sahl had come from Canada by way of failures to behave in the military and again in college. He performed for free in strip clubs to get to the stage at the hungry i, and he stacked his first audience with pals. He hid his reminders in a rolled-up newspaper, a prop that fit the shtick of talking about the news. Sahl's act was part of the "Broom Time" of comedy, sweeping away pretension and peeping under the covers and the cover-ups. Social satire, absurdist wit, existential jocularity, a funny fist-in-the-face—Sahl, Lenny Bruce and the other topical funny men of the period were the jaws of life in a time of political blacklisting—performers born of a roguish quarrelsomeness native to ethnic underclasses everywhere. Free speech has a price. When he was vocal in his distrust of the Warren Commission report on the assassination of President Kennedy, it cost Sahl most of his audience and income. It was up to you to stay or go. Wherever you were seated, among whatever numbers, Sahl was speaking directly to you. Tragedy is universal, but comedy is personal.

CM:
Feverish

A Hunger Artist, Franz Kafka, 1922. He saw Milena for the last time in May, not long after writing the title story of his last authorized book, and when the Workman's Insurance Accident Institute pensioned him off the next month he moved into a country house rented by his sister for the summer, confiding that he felt "like someone expelled from the world." He blamed his insomnia on writing; also his fevers. But sometimes when he read his work to friends he doubled over in laughter, so his decision to cast butchers as the permanent watchers of the hunger artist must have delighted him. Declining interest in public fasts is what leads the hunger artist to perform in a cage at the circus, where the crowd prefers the menagerie. There is no accounting for taste. The panther installed in the cage after the artist's death came from the zoo in Paris, which inspired Rilke's *New Poems*. The image locked in its heart? A dying man pursing his lips, as if to kiss the overseer who ordered the cage to be cleared. Kafka abandoned *The Castle* at the end of the summer, nevertheless preserving a copy for Milena. Like his sisters, she did not escape the camps, the construction of which Kafka foresaw in his fiction. She came to mind this morning, as I was counting out my pills after another sleepless night, unable to remember if I had taken them yesterday and also unnerved by the realization that two of my friends who had tried to starve themselves to death bore the names of my wife and younger daughter—a strange conjunction of facts that on another day I might have dismissed. What courage Milena displayed in a darkening world, what love.

MB:
Soldier Aristotle

"Among School Children," William Butler Yeats, 1928. The site of a famous typographical error that first appeared in his *Collected Poems* in 1933 and was replicated thereafter for fourteen years. Of course, Yeats meant "*solider* Aristotle." One imagines the drudgery and busy-work suggested by the fiction of Aristotle's military mind. Aristotle at the beginning, the middle and the end, advancing on the battle-field of thinkers. As between Plato and Aristotle, Yeats preferred the latter's assertion of a here-and-now reality, though it provided him no solace. Yeats is undergoing a personal age of anxiety in the poem, a senior citizen standing among children. Having turned sixty in 1925, and a senator, he tours a County Waterford elementary school in 1926. He would live to seventy-four, but is already at sixes and sevens, largely because he didn't get the girl. His Leda is not that swan-for-a-god, but the Ledaean Maud Gonne. Living at Thoor Ballylee, he includes the poem in *The Tower* in 1928. On May 26, 2014, Memorial Day, I thought again of Yeats, great by the standards of art, yet feeling defeated by the years. The radio was broadcasting Rosemary Clooney, once billed as "the girl singer," singing wistfully of time: you're young—stop, turn around—you're old. I have no-ticed that any conversation with my son instantaneously wipes away the sadness one cannot but feel as one ages. Yeats, having experienced the heat of his youthful poetry, still cradling the embers of unre-quited love—Yeats stands bent, a great poet by every standard except that which thinks art is an answer.

CM:
The Headless Horseman

"The Lady with the Little Dog," Anton Chekhov, 1899. By the time Dmitri Gurov realizes that a seemingly inconsequential affair begun in Yalta has turned serious, it is too late for him to change course. Anna Seegeenva, with her beret and white Pomeranian, has captured his heart: nothing will ever be the same. Once, in a graduate seminar on the literature of difficult love, the poet-professor noted that when Gurov, desperate to see Anna, travels to the provincial town of S. and takes a room in the hotel there is on the dusty table "an ink-stand, with a horseback rider, who held his hat in his raised hand, but whose head was broken off"—a detail long overlooked by the poet-professor until another writer pointed it out to him. So knowledge is passed from one artist to another, and for years I consigned this piece of wisdom to the realm of craft—a technical matter. One morning in Moscow, though, leaving my hotel with a heavy heart, I saw a bouquet of flowers above the entrance to the block of flats in the lift of which the journalist Anna Politkovskaya was shot and killed; for some reason this offering made in her memory brought me to my senses, and for the rest of my journey I registered my surroundings knowing that what Gurov and Anna discover at the end of the story—"the most complicated and difficult part was just beginning"—did not apply to you and me. The old theme of hopeless love. Politkovskaya's reporting on crimes committed by Russian soldiers in Chechnya irked the authorities, who may have had a hand in her assassination. How hard it is to see the truth.

MB:

Dolly

July 5, 1996, the birth of Dolly, a native of Edinburgh, the original cloned sheep, who would live past six and a half. The cell used to create this Dolly came from a mammary gland, which inspired the happy cloners to name her after the well-endowed country singer Dolly Parton. It is a heartfelt music that suffers neither irony nor disbelief. Dolly the sheep gave birth to Bonnie, the twins Sally and Rosie, and the triplets Lucy, Darcy and Cotton. As W. H. Auden said of the kinds of lakes among which one might choose a lake to own, "Just reeling off their names is ever so comfy." If I go literary to characterize the turn of mind that writes its own script, I do so because we have gone forth headlong in the material sciences, leaving the understanding of ourselves to the abstraction of alphabets and the slant light of postscripts. There may come people who will live forever, for whom we will clone, grow or manufacture every replacement part. Such people will wonder what it was like to have been mortal. For now, there can be no rapprochement between those who believe and those who disbelieve, for both belief and disbelief are matters of faith. Montaigne: "We are, I know not how, double in ourselves, so that what we believe we disbelieve, and cannot rid ourselves of what we condemn." Just so, I am the detective of my memory, seeking the clues to how I became, over a lifetime, a wayward clone of my past. My friend Al and I, born the same year and close for over half a century, had planned to celebrate our one hundred and fiftieth birthday, but he didn't make it, and there is no one to take his place.

CM:
Effluent

Black Watch, Gregory Burke, 2006. We were ordering drinks at the Scotch Malt Whiskey Society in Edinburgh when my host recalled his father trying a single malt described as having the aroma and taste of industrial effluent. But what he chalked up to Scottish humor was truth in advertising—which was missing from the arguments made for the invasion of Iraq in 2003, the subject of the verbatim play I was to discuss at a conference on Scotland's place in the world. Three members of the Black Watch Regiment are killed in a suicide car bombing, and when the survivors recount their tour of duty to a writer in a pub things turn ugly. One soldier wounded in the attack reports that he kept re-breaking his arm so that he would not have to return to battle. "Better. Break it," he chants, closing in on the writer, his refrain bringing to mind the warnings that military action would break Iraq apart. The Scottish independence movement was gathering speed, and at the conference it was assumed that revenue from the North Sea oil reserves belonged to the Scots. No one thought that London would object. I took an interest in the Scottish programming on TV—part of my family had emigrated from Fife—without understanding a word of what was said. Nor did I imagine that one day I would travel to Baghdad to coordinate the staging of new plays by American and Iraqi writers on the theme of courage. There were rumors of civil war, car bombings, assassinations; after one meeting our security detail drove us into a traffic jam by a crowded market. I asked a diplomat, my control officer, if she thought the man tailing us along the sidewalk was a local intelligence asset or a spotter for the insurgents. She shook her head. We sat in silence for more than twenty minutes, until the traffic cleared. The man vanished into the crowd when we reached the road that led to the Tigris River, and it was not until we arrived at the embassy that the defense contractor in the passenger's seat turned around and said, *He's one of ours.*

MB:
Russell

Bertrand Russell, May 18, 1872–February 2, 1970. An event of mind that lasted almost ninety-eight years. We shall not see his kind again, but are beset by ideologues pretending to be thinkers. I was hurrying along Broadway in the Capitol Hill District of Seattle. As I sped past two men deeply engaged in conversation as they walked, my hand bumped the wrist of one. I glanced back to say "excuse me" and kept going. But the bump must have "cleared the wax from my ears," as our teachers used to put it, and I realized that the older of the two was talking about Albert Camus. He was talking about Camus, Existentialism and meaninglessness. That was the word he used: "meaninglessness." I had overheard him say that meaninglessness was "a big idea." I couldn't just keep going. I went back and confirmed that they were indeed discussing Camus. I asked if they knew his essay on the myth of Sisyphus, who was sentenced to eternally push a boulder up to the top of a hill from where it would always roll down again. The older man (the other was much younger) said that in fact he had just been talking about Sisyphus. So I asked if he knew the very last sentence in the essay. "It's very important," I said, trying not to wag my finger. Well, he didn't, and he looked as if he wanted me to tell him, and I did. The last sentence in Camus' essay, the last of Camus' ideas about this man Sisyphus—who has been sentenced to an eternity of what seems to be meaningless suffering—is, "One must imagine Sisyphus happy." The older man was delighted at this information, and the younger one's eyes lit up as if he had been given permission to be cheerful. I felt like a Boy Scout of philosophy. I hadn't helped anyone across the street. I hadn't offered a way to escape the dark matter and sticky stuff. I had simply pointed out that one could live there. And I have lived there myself, largely as a fly on the wall, a bystander at the parties of the famous, a guest whose photo was taken in the movie star's bathtub, a tourist in international hot spots. We date watersheds, ages and eras, firsts and lasts, but nothing is over until no one remembers. Blessings on the lone scholar who looks again and recovers our words. Nonetheless, I have, like Bertrand Russell, no illusions.

CM:
The Dolly Zoom

Vertigo, Alfred Hitchcock, 1958. We were saving up for the wedding, in a flat on Capitol Hill, and though my paycheck from the nursery did not go far I still imagined our future as a golden thread. Rain was my constant companion as I shoveled bark onto trucks, sold azaleas, planted ornamental trees in the developments encircling Seattle. One day, pounding rebar into a railroad tie, I fell to my knees, queasy from a bout of vertigo, which came on suddenly and lasted for weeks. "A preview of marriage?" I joked. Sometimes I feel as if I have been spinning ever since. Hitchcock used a dolly zoom to film his ghost story, continuously distorting perspective to create what became known as the *Vertigo* effect. The formula for the film, he said, was "boy meets girl, boy loses girl, boy meets girl again, boy loses girl again"—which you could call the story of my life. Frames within frames. Jimmy Stewart follows Kim Novak down the streets of San Francisco, into an alley, and enters a dark passageway that opens onto a flower shop, the light from which overwhelms him. The orchids in the greenhouse were as intoxicating to me as the memory of my last morning in the Presidio, when we ran to the Golden Gate Bridge and back. At the midpoint of the film the stars drive to Muir Woods, and there they gaze at the cross-section of a tree felled twenty-five years before, with a series of white rings indicating significant moments in history—the Battle of Hastings, the signing of the Magna Carta, the discovery of America. She traces her finger over the rings between her birth and looming death, murmuring, *You took no notice.* Her feigned madness inflames his imagination. *You see,* he tells her later, in the stable at the Spanish mission, *there's an answer for everything.* If he only knew.

MB:
Guff and Jive

Monday, May 28, 1956, publication of Colin Wilson's *The Outsider*. Or should I have dated it Christmas Day, 1954, when Wilson first wrote in his journal "Notes for a book The Outsider in Literature . . . "? I read it new, half a year from college. I had a habit of separating what people said from what they meant, which did not lessen my small town naïveté. Wilson did not write of public discourse, but of the personal condition of the outsider. Years later, I asked Edmund Wilson, to whom the book was dedicated, to tell me about Colin Wilson—which seemed to dismay him, who no doubt expected my interest to be in himself. I grew up anti-poetic and would never have written poetry but for the Beats, unfit as I was for the preciousness of high culture. I was so ill-read outside of schoolwork that I had to invent a novel to review for the New York State regents examination. I was so focused elsewhere during school time that I had to call for more paper so I could solve trig problems without the trigonometric tables. I ad-libbed an education, emptied my head after tests, and considered philosophy to be my life's work. Of course, Wilson's happy "synthesis," resting on the rose-tinted glasses provided by the sweet and sad beauties of art, is guff and jive that, like a spoonful of honey, makes the medicine go down. I was not immune. In my psychological safe room, lifted by sentimental ballads and jazz, I loved Clyde McCoy's 1930's wah-wah, flutter-tongue rendition of "Sugar Blues." The title said it all.

CM:
Medicine

"Different Drum," The Stone Poneys, 1967. Their only hit launched the career of Linda Ronstadt, who stood now, in July 2014, in the East Room of the White House for the entrance of the President and the First Lady. Obama's remarks on the centrality to our lives of the arts and humanities concluded with a story of Lincoln presenting the Emancipation Proclamation to his Cabinet. It seems that he began the meeting by reading aloud a chapter from the humorist Artemus Ward's *High-Handed Outrage at Utica*, at the end of which he laughed and laughed. His Cabinet remained silent. So he read another chapter. More silence. Lincoln closed the book. "Gentlemen," he said, "why don't you laugh? You need this medicine as much as I do." Obama joked with the artists and scholars before presenting them with medals honoring their determination to follow their own paths, and when he confessed to once having had a crush on the singer who lost her voice to Parkinson's disease the room swelled with laughter. The ceremony must have been a relief for him. He was coming from a video conference with European leaders to discuss imposing more sanctions on Russia, and his diplomatic efforts in the Middle East were failing. Israeli forces had bombed a school in Gaza, Hamas was about to release a video of militants emerging from a tunnel dug near a kibbutz to mount a surprise attack, and the Islamic State was advancing on Baghdad, from which a poet sent me an inscrutable couplet requesting that I edit his translation. The last line of "Different Drum" was running through my mind: "We'll both live a lot longer if you live without me." Mike Nesmith, who wrote the song before he joined The Monkees, is still performing. Linda Ronstadt never married.

MB:
Happiness

July 17, 1996, TWA flight 800 crashes into the Atlantic Ocean near East Moriches, New York. It went into the water eight miles out from the Coast Guard Station to which, as a boy, I pedaled, my bicycle on weekends. I looked forward to racing past the duck pond under an umbrella of native maples and free-wheeling the quiet streets toward the water, satisfied to have a turnaround rather than a destination. This was the crux of my joy. I was a small-towner whose happiness was being alone with his thoughts and then making fun of them with friends on a battered launch site at the edge of the Bay. I knew a lot more than I was saying, but it was useless knowledge. How was I to help my father when I found him clutching a tree? The heart doctor told him to sell his store and he did, only to buy it back because being in the store made him happy. That taught me that happiness is a decision. Go away into art, philosophy and food, lose oneself on a bike on back roads, make fun of anything this side of abuse or deprivation. The eastern Long Islanders sped out in their jury-rigged clammers and weekend outboards to rescue passengers and were heartbroken to find no one to save. Afterward, the highways were a corridor of grief and blessings on crude signs that would hold happiness at bay for more than a year for a people who, like most others, did not easily live alone. I had yet to learn that a collaboration of two changes both.

CM:
The Ladder

"Untitled," Donald Judd, 1966. The overtly Islamic content of the international poster biennale, which occupied most of the galleries in Tehran's Museum of Contemporary Art in September 2009, made the construction jutting from the wall of the atrium all the more intriguing: nine panels of galvanized iron stacked one on top of another—boxes containing air and light, a ladder propped between the abyss and eternity. In the lull between the summer's post-electoral protests and the reopening of the universities for the fall term, I studied my countryman's work, which had survived the Iranian revolution, perhaps because it was too difficult to remove. (The bulk of the largest collection of modern Western art in Asia was locked away in the museum vault.) The critical view of Judd's spare geometric shapes as an attack on hierarchy, detached from history, I regarded as a continuation of Walt Whitman's democratic aesthetic: "Unscrew the locks from the doors!" the poet commands, summoning the forbidden voices of prisoners and slaves, of thieves and dwarfs, to articulate a vision of the universe in which everyone is connected to everything. The voices that he clarifies and transfigures belong to the living and the dead, inflected by the light traveling toward us from an explosion at the beginning of time, which will continue until the very end. I hold in my hand a postcard from an exhibit in Iowa City of Judd's drawings of rectangles, and as I prepare to return to the Islamic Republic to discuss a new collaboration, as yet untitled, which will surely change us for better or worse, let me just say after the fact: *Thank you.*

CHRISTOPHER MERRILL's recent books include *Boat* (poetry), *Necessities* (prose poetry), and *The Tree of the Doves: Ceremony, Expedition, War* (non-fiction). His work has been translated into nearly forty languages, and as the director of the International Writing Program at the University of Iowa he has conducted cultural diplomacy missions in more than fifty countries.

MARVIN BELL's works include collaborations with musicians, composers, dancers, poets and photographers—among them, poet William Stafford and photographer Nathan Lyons—and volumes of an original poetic form most recently collected in *Vertigo: The Living Dead Man Poems*. He lives in Iowa City, Iowa, and Port Townsend, Washington, and teaches for the brief-residency MFA program located in Oregon at Pacific University.